# Get the Best Out of the Rest of Your Life

Questions and answers on health, family, relationships, work and retirement, and money.

# Get the Best Out of the Rest of Your Life

A woman's guide to the second half of life

**Jean Shapiro**

Thorsons Publishing Group

First published 1990

© JEAN SHAPIRO 1990

British Library Cataloguing in Publication Data

Shapiro, Jean, *1916-*
  Get the best out of the rest of your life
  a woman's guide to the second half of life
  1. Middle age. Personal adjustment
  I. Title
  305.2'44

  ISBN 0-7225-1971-0

*Published by Thorsons Publishers Limited,*
*Wellingborough, Northamptonshire NN8 2RQ, England*

Typeset by Harper Phototypesetters Limited, Northampton
Printed in Great Britain by Mackays of Chatham, Kent

10  9  8  7  6  5  4  3  2

# Contents

# Introduction

When did you last see a television advertisement or a fashion photograph featuring a normal, attractive middle-aged or older woman? If women in their middle years, and especially elderly women, are shown at all, they're occasionally over-glamourized like a *Dynasty* star, but much more often characterized as comic cleaning ladies, feather-brained ditherers or intimidating mothers-in-law. Are we really like that?

If it's true to say that women have a long way to go before being really accepted as equal citizens, for women past their forties the disadvantages are even greater. Although we're an increasingly numerous group as the population in general lives longer, we're no less 'invisible' than we've ever been. Flick through a woman's magazine and you'll wonder what the clothes shown on the impossibly skinny models have got to do with you, let alone the millions of other women – a majority of the female population – who are size 14 or over. And how many novels have you read, how many films have you seen, in which there's a credible, living, breathing, loving middle-aged woman as heroine? There are very few.

Woman's traditional role as mother, housewife, carer hasn't really changed. Younger women may be struggling to combine their job outside the home with their job as the major carer within it; their mothers or their older sisters (except during war-time) have always been expected to put their families first. For years they've seen their job as looking after the needs of other people; they're the ones who are always there to wipe away the tears, soothe fevered brows, do battle with unfair teachers, have a hot meal ready

however inconvenient the time, shop and clean, and listen
to everyone's troubles. If they had a job at all, it was a *little*
one – chosen because the hours fitted in with the
family's, not because it was interesting or challenging –
which often had to be given up in a family crisis. Many
older women have never had any money they could really
call their own: money for necessities, let alone treats, had
to be saved out of the 'housekeeping' or begged for as a
special favour.

It's no wonder so many women over 40 have lost
confidence in themselves as people in their own right. And
sadly, because they haven't been able to believe in
themselves as more than 'John's wife' or 'Sally's mother',
both John and Sally have accepted them at their own low
self-evaluation. They're not expected to join in 'adult'
conversation or have valid political opinions, or to
understand the needs and aspirations of an older teenager.
They're out of touch, 'past it'.

Most women have accepted the world's, and their own,
negative view of themselves for so long that there are few
role models within their communities with whom to
identify. Although we can't necessarily emulate the
director or the TV star or other high-status women, we still
don't have to accept that lack of education and lack of
opportunity mean that we can't be successful at *anything*.
Our life experience, our ability to deal with a-hundred-and-
one domestic and family problems, our flexibility and
versatility, ought to make us valuable to a wider
community. In past centuries, as in some societies today,
'elders' of both sexes were respected; their wisdom was
called on in times of dispute or crisis. And, far from being
downgraded, older people were granted the privileges they
had earned.

That's a role we should reclaim. There are signs that, as
the numbers of young people available for work decline in
the 1990s, middle-aged and older people will be
increasingly wooed back into the labour market. This is an
opportunity that should be seized. Not since World War II
have women aged 40+ been so sought after and respected
for their contribution to the economy. It's up to us now to
see that if the situation changes (and there are signs that
the birthrate is going up again) we will never again be

persuaded that our duty's done, and that a woman's place, after all, is in the home. While we can, we should make sure that our needs, and those of the younger women who will come after us, are fully met. Flexible hours, communal services, better provision for the care of the old and disabled, nurseries and after-school facilities should be there for women of all ages as of right.

Regaining confidence, learning to work towards independence both emotional and financial – these are among the important topics that this book will try to address. The questions, and the answers, in the chapters that follow are based on the many thousands of letters I've received in more than twenty years as a magazine advice columnist. Magazine 'aunties' are asked about everything under the sun, and in our personal replies we draw on many sources, not the least of which are the experiences of our readers as well as our own filing systems and the facts we hold in our heads. Although the agony aunt is popularly believed to be concerned only with the teens and twenties and their romantic and sexual problems, that's far from the truth. Worried, depressed, anxious and unsure women of all ages from adolescence to the eighties write for information, reassurance, and moral support. A few men write too, on their own behalf as well as their partners'.

In our letters, and in this book, we avoid telling our readers what to do. Our job, I think, is to open up the options, to suggest possibilities the reader may have lost sight of, and only to give firm advice when the question is one of *fact*. I'd never tell a reader 'you ought to get a divorce'; but I would tell her how to contact her nearest counselling service and suggest books she could read to find out more about a certain job or career.

The chapter headings will steer you towards the questions that most closely resemble yours. It might then be useful to read the whole chapter, and the relevant booklist at the end of it and, if appropriate, to contact an organization for more information on your particular problem. When you see an asterisk * in the text following a group's title, this indicates that the organization's address and telephone number are listed in the Useful addresses section that begins on p.133.

# 1 Health and fitness

**Q** My mother is 71 and she suffers from all sorts of ailments which seem to be due to her age. I'm 40 and I don't want to be crippled with arthritis, or have a 'heart condition' when I'm her age. But aren't such things inevitable?

**A** Some of the health problems we develop as we get older can be attributed to heredity, but few of them to 'old age' as such. So much depends on the way we have looked after ourselves in our middle years – even how we lived in our teens and twenties. There's nothing that can be done to change our heredity. But by adhering to quite simple health rules all our lives, we can not only prevent many troubles in later years, but even affect the influence that heredity may play in the development of some diseases.

So don't accept that just because your mother has these conditions at 71, you will too. There are plenty of women a lot older than your mother who are active, healthy, mentally alert. You can look forward to a much happier old age than she is experiencing – but only if you act *now*. We know so much more about healthy living than we did when your mother was young; medical advances have also helped to prolong our active lives. If you take advantage of the information and advice that's freely on offer now, there's every reason to think that you can look forward to your seventies and eighties. But it's still largely up to you.

Q **There's been a lot of publicity about osteoporosis recently. Some doctors are in favour of hormone replacement therapy, others not. Aren't there some more natural ways of preventing it?**

A HRT, as it's generally known, *is* controversial. Some experts say that since osteoporosis is such a scourge, and can affect as many as a quarter of women over 70, every woman at or around the menopause should be put on to HRT. If that were done, they say, future generations wouldn't suffer this crippling degenerative disease.

The reason why some older women may be at risk of developing osteoporosis is that after the menopause, or after a total hysterectomy (where both ovaries are also removed), their bodies cease to produce the amount of oestrogen that younger women produce. Oestrogen appears to have an effect on maintaining bone density, and osteoporosis is a loss of bone density, resulting in easily-fractured bones and the spinal condition known as dowager's hump. The advocates of HRT say that *replacement* of the lost hormone prevents this bone loss.

In the early days of hormone replacement therapy, when oestrogen alone was given, it was found that some women who still retained their wombs developed cancer of the endometrium (lining of the womb). Always more popular in the United States than in Britain, HRT thus got a bad name and many women refused treatment. Later research showed that adding progestogen to the treatment cycle prevented endometrial cancer, and the way was open once more for advocates of the therapy to stress its advantages and discount any possible disadvantages. Foremost among those advocates, of course, were the drug companies who would benefit enormously if all middle-aged and older women were treated with HRT for the rest of their lives.

All this is very confusing to the ordinary woman who is the target of the information and hype that comes at her from the media, her doctor and some organizations. So let's try to sort out the pros and cons.

First, the advantages:

+ It does seem certain that HRT can prevent osteoporosis or lessen its effects if it is begun at the onset of the menopause and continued for the rest of our lives.
+ Some women claim that HRT makes them feel better in general, and that it can improve skin texture and their appearance, though many authorities who are in favour of HRT for the prevention of osteoporosis don't lay claim to these extra benefits.
+ Now that HRT normally includes progestogen, there is actually a *protective* effect on the lining of the womb.
+ There have been some claims that HRT lessens the likelihood of heart disease.

Now the disadvantages:

– Only 25 per cent of women will develop osteoporosis. Since we can predict with some certainty who is really at risk, it may be wasteful of resources to give HRT to the 75 per cent who are not at risk.
– Progestogen, now included in HRT, *may* be linked with the development of breast cancer. The treatment has not been available long enough for anyone to be sure that there won't be other bad effects in the long run. In 1988 some research showed that women taking the contraceptive pill were much more likely to develop breast cancer than non-pill takers.

However, it may be that since the HRT 'pill'
has rather different constituents, these
unconfirmed findings may not apply.
  −   Many women dislike having a monthly
period-like bleeding for the rest of their lives –
it's bothersome and seems unnatural for a
post-menopausal woman.

For the individual trying to decide whether HRT
is indicated in her particular case, there are a few
guidelines. If she suffers from certain medical
problems, her doctors will not prescribe HRT in
any case. If her mother, aunts or sisters have lived
into old age without developing osteoporosis, the
chances are strongly in favour of her not
developing the problem, either. If she's large-boned
and not underweight (actually a little plump) she's
likely to be protected. If she's black, she has little
to fear, since osteoporosis is almostly entirely
confined to people of European or Asian origin.
Finally, there is a scanning technique now widely
available in the US, but not yet widespread under
the NHS in Britain (it's expensive) which can
predict the likelihood of any individual developing
osteoporosis in later years. One can't help feeling
that British National Health Service money
would be better spent detecting those at risk than
in funding the provision of HRT to the 75 per
cent of women who won't need it.
    You ask whether there isn't a more 'natural'
way of preventing osteoporosis. Of course those
who support HRT say that *it* is natural, since it's
simply replacing a natural substance in the
female body that is no longer produced in large
enough quantity to prevent osteoporosis. But
there is evidence that regular exercise (not
necessarily *exercises*) helps maintain bone
density. Since we may start to lose a little bone
from our thirties onwards, both men (who are not
at such risk as women, but who do sometimes
develop osteoporosis in old age) and women
should make sure they walk for at least half an

hour a day, remain active in other ways, practise weight-bearing jobs such as carrying shopping bags to keep their arms working, and avoid staying in bed except for really severe illnesses. A recent report in the *British Medical Journal* showed that a group of elderly people who took regular exercise suffered from fewer fractured femurs than did their peers who were relatively inactive.

Diet is probably very important, too. Although there is a lot of controversy about the role of calcium in preventing osteopososis, it seems likely that a calcium-rich diet may help, so whatever your age you should include milk, cheese, yoghurt, etc, in your daily diet, along with green vegetables, sesame seeds and wholemeal bread, and encourage your daughters to do likewise. In fact, like everyone else, a woman who wants to do the best she can to avoid osteoporosis in her later years should adopt the healthy lifestyle outlined in answers to the questions that follow in this chapter.

The National Osteoporosis Society* in Britain provides information and advice on the condition. Although its literature does recommend calcium-rich diets and exercise, it appears to have a bias in favour of hormone treatment. The Amarant Trust,* backed by experts working in conjunction with some pharmaceutical companies on research and treatment, favours HRT for all women who want it, unless there are medical contra-indications. The Women's Association for Research in Menopause* is a good source of information in the US.

Q **I have clear signs of arthritis in my hands and knees. My doctor tells me there's no treatment – he just offers painkillers. Is there anything I can do to prevent it getting worse?**

A There are basically two kinds of arthritis – rheumatoid arthritis and osteoarthritis. Since a majority of older people do develop some form of osteoarthritis, this is probably what your doctor means when he confirms the diagnosis of arthritis. It often shows itself first in one or two fingers, with slight almost painless swellings in the 'top' joints. Later, other joints – hips, knees and ankles – may be affected. Movement is very painful and becomes increasingly restricted. The condition is caused by wear and tear – the cartilage in the joint has been gradually worn away.

Rheumatoid arthritis is a disease that affects the whole body. The lining of the joint capsule (the synovial membrane) becomes inflamed, and this produces substances (enzymes) that damage cartilage, bone, and soft tissue, even, in bad cases, destroying the affected joint. It can occur at any age, but about half the women who have it are over 50.

Both kinds of arthritis can be helped, and anyone who has osteoarthritis is especially able to help herself. Doctors do prescribe painkillers, and some of these – aspirin, for instance – help to treat the condition as well as lessen the pain. The disadvantage of aspirin is that it sometimes causes stomach irritation so, if you can't tolerate aspirin, your GP can prescribe another drug.

However, the very best treatment is a sensible combination of rest and exercise. Some sufferers find that daily joint exercise, undertaken first thing in the morning, loosens the joints and makes normal activities almost completely pain-free. Every joint in turn should be gently rotated or moved up and down until it reaches its limit. And you should gently stretch arms, legs and back a few times a day; avoid remaining too long in one position; and if you're at all overweight, try to reduce *gradually*, as carrying a lot of bodyweight can add to the wear and tear on hip joints. Try to keep warm; walk as briskly as you can several times a week. These self-help measures should keep you mobile for far longer that if you just accepted the 'nothing can be done' approach.

People with advanced arthritis may be offered surgery – hip and knee replacements are the most common operations. Over 120,000 of these operations are done each year in the US. In Britain there is a notoriously long waiting list for NHS joint-replacement operations. Results of these operations are usually good, at least in the short term. A replacement can wear out in 10-15 years; faster if the person is very much overweight. The operation carries the same risks as any operation (post-operative infections and the possibility of blood clots) but as long as you are able to tolerate anaesthesia and you're not too much overweight, the operation can be successful at any age.

In the UK, Arthritis Care* runs many local support groups and the Arthritis and Rheumatism Council* provides information and funds research. In the US the Arthritis Foundation* has local chapters, publishes information and has developed guidelines for underwater exercises. The Arthritis Information Clearing House offers materials and bibliographies.

Q I've just discovered a small lump in my breast. I'm too scared to go to the doctor. I suppose I'd rather die than face a mutilating operation.

A First of all, remember that by no means all breast lumps are cancerous. If yours isn't, knowing so would take a great weight off your mind.

Secondly, if the small lump is cancer, the sooner it is diagnosed and treated, the less likely you are to need the mastectomy operation you dread.

If and when breast screening by mammography is offered to every middle-aged woman in the UK on the NHS (as has been promised) early detection may mean that mastectomy is outdated.

There is some controversy about the advantages of 'lumpectomy' (removal of just the small growth, leaving the breast intact) versus mastectomy (removal of the whole breast). Anyone whose breast cancer is far advanced, however, will really have no choice – one good reason for regular self-examination of the breasts so that an abnormality can be spotted early. Women with smaller tumours and no evidence that the cancer has spread do have a choice, and they should inform themselves of the pros and cons and exercise that choice. Removal of the tumour only may also involve post-operative radio- or chemotherapy. Some women will still prefer to have a mastectomy, because they feel that this is more likely to deal once and for all with the problem; and there are very many women alive today who had mastectomies many years ago and have had no recurrence of cancer. Others will take note of the figures that tend to show that the outcome of a lumpectomy is no worse than that of mastectomy, when the usual five-year survival rate is taken into account. If you're faced with this choice, do take time to decide. Don't agree that if an exploratory operation reveals cancer the surgeon should immediately proceed with a mastectomy. It's your body, and you should be consulted. Delay of a week or two won't affect the outcome, and it will give you time to talk to the consultant, your own doctor and anyone else likely to offer you information.

Of course if a mastectomy seems the right procedure for you, it's very hard to come to terms with the loss of such a vital part of your body. As with any severe personal loss, the emotional healing takes time. Some hospitals offer a counselling service: ask about this. And there are voluntary groups, run by women who have had mastectomies, who will visit patients in hospital and when they return home, keeping in touch as long as necessary to ease the mental pain and showing, by their own example, how it is possible to accept what has happened and lead happy and productive lives despite their loss. The Breast Care and Mastectomy Association* and BACUP* in the UK, the Cancer Information Service* and the National Cancer Survivors Network* in the US are the organizations to contact. You may also consider the merits of a breast prosthesis, or a breast reconstruction operation. Get all the information you can.

Some other forms of cancer are less easily diagnosed and treated. If you have another form of cancer, or someone close to you is affected, some of the books listed on page 140 will help you. Most cancer today is treated by surgery plus radiotherapy or chemotherapy. Side-effects can be very unpleasant, but most doctors would say that despite these, the eventual outcome is positive enough to be worth the problems encountered while the treatment is undergone.

A 'holistic' approach is offered by bodies such as the Bristol Cancer Help Centre* in the UK which aims to offer alternative methods of care for sufferers through diet, meditation and lifestyle changes. *Care Services in the USA* by Shirley Linde and Donald J. Carrow contains addresses of holistic health care practitioners in the US.

**Q** **At 44 my husband has just been told he has heart disease. Isn't that terribly young? And what can he expect in the future?**

**A** Sadly, it's not very unusual nowadays for someone in his forties to develop heart trouble. Someone who smokes, drinks or eats too much (particularly foods high in animal fats) and doesn't take enough exercise is a candidate for heart disease. Stress may also play a part; and of course if heart trouble runs in the family, that can be a major factor too. What happens is that the coronary arteries have become narrowed by a build-up of cholesterol; the condition is made even worse when the effect of inhaled smoke contracts the arteries still further. If a clot or small fragment of cholesterol becomes detached and reaches the heart, it can temporarily or permanently affect heart function.

Given the probable cause, it's obvious what the preventative measures are. Your husband should try very hard to stop smoking. Of course it's very difficult to kick the habit – some say it's as hard to come off cigarettes as to come off hard drugs. While he's going through the withdrawal period, he'll need every possible support from the family. He may become very irritable, nervous, tense and difficult to live with. He should talk to his doctor about any local 'stop smoking' groups and get literature from ASH* in the UK or US.

The link between alcohol and heart disease is less clear, but there is some evidence that over-indulgence can contribute. Your husband should observe the 'safe-drinking' guidelines – one glass of wine, or one measure of spirits or half a pint of beer is the daily maximum – but he should consult his doctor.

If he is overweight he should undertake a weight-reduction programme, aiming at losing not more than one pound a week (see page 26). He should cut down on fatty foods, avoid fried foods altogether, cut visible fat off meat, and cut down on red meat. He should eat plenty of fish (there's a lot of evidence that oily *fish*, as distinct from fatty meat, has a beneficial effect), eat no more than three eggs a week (including those 'invisible' eggs in baked goods, puddings, etc.) He should increase his intake of vegetables and fruit and use them as 'fillers' if his reduced diet leaves him hungry. Semi-skimmed milk and polyunsaturated margarine should partially replace full-cream milk and butter.

These changes in diet are quite easily achieved by many people, and of course they can be beneficial to the whole family, so that having to prepare special meals for your husband won't be a problem. Although women up to the age of the menopause suffer far fewer heart attacks than men, in their later years, unfortunately, they catch up, and so are at as much risk. If you (or your husband) are particularly fond of fatty foods and eat a lot of meat and eggs, and you do find it hard to cut down on these, I'd suggest you do so gradually. It's wonderful how quickly we can adapt to changes in diet if we're really motivated, as anyone who has given up sugar in tea or coffee can tell you. After a few weeks you'll be surprised that you ever seemed to need so much fatty food, and will enjoy preparing and eating some of the meals taken from the recipe books listed on pages 32 and 33.

Q   **I have high blood-pressure and I know that this means I am at risk of a stroke. How should I change my lifestyle to make this less likely?**

A   Longstanding hypertension (high blood-pressure) is the main cause of a stroke. A stroke results when the blood vessels supplying oxygen to the brain are blocked, as when the arteries are 'silted up' with deposits of cholesterol. A clot, or embolism, lodges in one of these narrowed arteries, blocking the blood flow, and the artery bursts. The brain is flooded with blood from this artery, which cuts down the blood flow to the brain and puts pressure on it. Diabetic people are particularly at risk if they are also hypertensive.

In severe cases of high blood-pressure, a doctor will usually prescribe drugs which reduce the pressure but, as with all medication, there can be undesirable side-effects. Self-help measures are exactly the same as those outlined in the answer to the previous question, plus reduction of salt in the diet. Add little or no salt to your cooking, and don't put a salt cellar on the table.

Since you are at risk, you should be aware of the possible symptoms of stroke, because sometimes a series of slight strokes precede a more serious one. The symptoms are:

severe and persistent headache;
temporary weakness or numbness in the limbs or face on one side of the body;
temporary loss or dimness of vision;
dizziness or unsteadiness;
loss of memory.

Each of these symptoms could be caused by other problems, but if you do experience them, and you have high blood-pressure, your doctor should be contacted at once.

Rehabilitation after a stroke depends on its severity, but the outlook is increasingly good and today even someone who has lost the use of an arm or leg or whose speech has been badly affected can be helped to regain some normal function by physiotherapy and occupational therapy, plus the co-operation of family and friends.

Information on prevention and treatment of strokes, including the Volunteer Stroke Scheme set up to help rehabilitate stroke sufferers with communication problems, are available from the Chest, Heart and Stroke Association.* The American Heart Association* has literature helpful to stroke sufferers and their families.

## Q What are the symptoms of diabetes?

A There are at least two types of diabetes, with
different causes. Type I is insulin-dependent and
Type II non insulin-dependent. Type I is usually
diagnosed in young people, while Type II used to
be called 'adult-onset' because it most often
affected middle-aged or older people. It's
increasingly prevalent today, probably because of
our unnatural diet and sedentary lifestyle.

In both types too little insulin is secreted in the
pancreas and this affects blood sugar. Type I
diabetics need to have this insulin replaced,
usually by regular injections. Type II people may
be prescribed medication to take by mouth, but in
the majority of cases they control their diabetes
by the sort of changes in diet and exercise that we
looked at on pages 20 and 21, plus a careful watch
on the calories, particularly those produced by
sugar and other carbohydrates. Anyone diagnosed
as diabetic should be given help by a dietician and
should arm him or herself with all the information provided by the British Diabetic Association* and the American Diabetes Association.*

Sometimes 'gestation diabetes' is found in
pregnant women, when it should be picked up by
routine blood tests. Although once the baby is
born things settle down, it is an early warning
that the woman is at risk of developing Type II
diabetes when she's older, so she should aim to
lose weight and watch her diet and exercise pattern.

The warning signs of all types of diabetes are:

fatigue;
increased thirst;
frequent passing of urine;
vaginal infections and itching;
poor healing of minor wounds;
weight gain or rapid weight loss;
poor vision;
dental disease.

As you can see, most of these symptoms could be confused with 'getting older', but blood and urine tests will establish whether they're caused by diabetes or have some other significance. Because the symptoms are so vague, many people go undiagnosed for years until some symptom gives cause for concern.

Q **I hate looking older and the slowing up that seems to be happening. What can I do about it?**

A From the moment we're born we're getting older. For some of us it's difficult to accept that we're not as young-looking and active as we used to be. It's particularly hard if we've set great store by our looks, believing that our only real assets lie in a pretty face and a slim figure, so the loss of these makes us feel almost non-persons. Sadly, society, dominated as it is by male values, encourages us to believe in these transient assets and neglect the more lasting and positive ones that reside in what we *are* rather than how we *look*. Men don't expect to be judged and valued in those terms: the figures (or lack of them) that many men cut on any beach can be so gross that few women would be happy in equivalent beachwear. A woman who has 'let herself go' is derided; an overweight man is just accepted as middle-aged.

So the first step towards accepting the inevitable wrinkles and less-than-youthful figure is to learn to value ourselves as people who have far more to contribute than just adding to the decor. We all have abilities and talents – and most of us have far more skills than just the ability to hold the routine job we may have had in our youth. Anyone who has had a family to care for has become a versatile juggler with her time. Dealing with people and domestic problems has given her experience of life often more effective than all the theorists, experts and gurus put

together. A book like the one by Anne Dickson
(see page 45) can help us set a value on ourselves
far greater than the way we look. And how often
have you admired the poise, dignity and beauty
shown by a confident woman well past her youth?

All this doesn't mean you need pay no
attention to your appearance! For health as well as
for aesthetic reasons excess weight is undesirable.
A hairstyle that suits *your* face may bear only a
small resemblance to current fashion (though
you'll feel awkward if you retain a style that was
suitable in your twenties but is really dated now).
Grey hair is actually less ageing than artificial
colouring which can betray your lack of
confidence in yourself rather than deceive people
into subtracting a decade or two from your age.
As we get older we cannot erase wrinkles,
however much we pay for the latest cosmetic
creams or lotions, but our skins are often
uncomfortably dry, so that emollients or
moisturizers may be needed. It's tempting to use
as much make-up as we may have used twenty or
thirty years ago, but too much make-up disguises
nothing and can actually look grotesque. Less,
rather than more, should be the rule.

Diet and exercise can keep us healthier, more
supple, physically stronger, less liable to
degenerative disease, and make us look and feel
better. The guidelines are always the same: look
at pages 20 and 21. Exercising alone can be boring
and often counter-productive; if there's a keep-fit
class near you, and it's run by sensible people,
you'll not only benefit physically, but get a lot of
fun from being with your fellow-students. Ask at
your adult education centre or contact the Keep
Fit Association* in the UK or the YWCA in the
US.

Q    **How can I lose weight?**

First of all, be very sure that you really *are*
overweight. A few years ago the 'ideal weight'
tables accepted by medical and lay people were
revised in an upward direction. It's not now
regarded as a sign of health and fitness to be very
slim, and there's some evidence that being
slightly plump helps protect against osteoporosis,
so it's quite important for middle-aged women not
to aim to reduce weight drastically. Perhaps the
best guideline is to recall what your weight was
around age 21. Unless you were clearly too fat
then, that's probably a healthy weight for *you*.

But assuming you are a stone (14 lb/6.5 kg) or
more above your youthful weight, you probably do
want to lose a few pounds. Go at it gradually.
There's plenty of evidence to show that people
who undertake drastic diets not only starve
themselves of essential nutrients, but actually
tend to regain weight as soon as they go back to
normal eating. The reason is that the body gets
used to the reduced food intake, reprogrammes
itself to function on less food, and when the
amount is subsequently increased, the intake
actually constitutes *over*-eating. Thus weight is
rapidly regained and the dieter ends up after some
months even heavier than she was before. The
diet suggested on pages 20 and 21, combined with
exercise, will result in an overweight person
losing roughly 1 lb a week. That seems very little,
but if you're aiming to lose 14 lb, you'll achieve
that in a little over three months. Even more
important, you'll have achieved this while eating
healthily, and your body won't have been shocked
into adapting to a very low-calorie diet.

Until fairly recently it was believed that the
amount of exercise a person took had little
bearing on weight loss. Now it's been established
that although there is very little loss resulting
from a sudden, one-off bout of exercising, what

does have an effect is *regular* exercise. If you walk rather than catch a bus or drive, walk upstairs rather than use a lift, and make this a daily practice while at the same time changing to a healthy, rather than a 'slimming' diet, you won't need to reduce the amount of food you eat at all.

If you're unused to walking or climbing stairs, start gradually. Aim at a short walk to start with – say for 20 minutes on flat ground. Then begin to speed up so that you are walking briskly. Then increase the distance. Eventually you should be able to take a brisk walk at least three times a week, each walk lasting not less than half an hour. Apply the same principle to stair-climbing. Your heart as well as your figure will benefit.

For health reasons in general, a change of diet should involve eating less fat from animal sources, more fibre, less sugar and salt. The good news is that this healthy eating will result in weight loss in a person who has previously been eating too many of the *unhealthy* foods.

Some large women have rejected the whole concept of being overweight and have formed the Fat Women's Support Group.*

Q **All the experts say we should change our diet and exercise habits. But my family are stuck in their ways. My husband insists on bacon and eggs for breakfast, the children live on chips. None of them will walk anywhere if they can cadge a ride.**

A Changing the habits of a lifetime is hard for some people. Only two things seem to affect them. The first is, unfortunately, personal experience of the damage they may be doing themselves by persisting in eating unhealthy foods. A man whose doctor warns him very seriously that his heart is at risk, *and explains to him very clearly* just what the build-up of cholesterol in his arteries can result in, may take heed having previously ignored nagging or vague exhortations to change his diet. He is even more likely to change his ways if a friend or relative whose lifestyle was similar to his own suffers a heart attack or stroke.

The other approach is to adopt dietary changes gradually. Many people actually don't mind substituting polyunsaturated margarine for butter, semi-skimmed milk for full-fat in tea, attractive baked fish dishes and well-chosen vegetarian meals for meat a couple of times a week. At first preparing such meals may be more time consuming than grilling a fatty chop or picking up a fish-and-chip supper; but with practice, and a certain amount of planning, really tasty meals aren't difficult to produce, and add a welcome variety to the family diet.

Encouraging people to take exercise is sometimes harder. Joining an exercise class or a sports club can provide an incentive. And what's wrong with refusing a teenager a lift in the car when the alternative is a mile's walk?

**Q** **Health food shops and chemists are full of vitamin pills. Should I be taking supplements, and if so, which?**

**A** Medical opinion has mostly subscribed to the belief that no-one whose diet is well-balanced, with plenty of protein, carbohydrates and a reduced amount of fat, needs to worry about extras. An exception is sometimes made for older people for whom some doctors believe that a daily multi-vitamin pill can be helpful.

Of course health food shops, pharmaceutical companies and other interests want to persuade us that we need supplements, so their hype must be viewed with some scepticism. Against this, however, there are two factors. First, the recommended daily allowance (RDA) of many vitamins and minerals varies from country to country. In Britain, for instance, officially recommended allowances of some vitamins are less than those recommended in the United States; and the amount of calcium recommended for pregnant women is substantially lower than the amounts considered necessary in the Soviet Union and the United States. Second, the balanced diet we should all be consuming includes such items as fresh, preferably uncooked, vegetables and fruit. But how many of us have access to really fresh produce, uncontaminated by pesticides and other chemicals?

Supplements are expensive, so no-one wants to buy unnecessary pills and capsules, and of course huge overdoses of vitamins A and D (which are not water-soluble) can actually be dangerous. (The water-soluble B and C vitamins don't present problems of overdosing, because excess is excreted in urine.)

Perhaps the best course is to make sure that your diet includes adequate amounts of: protein (lean meat and fish, eggs, beans and pulses, dairy products); wholemeal bread, brown rice, oat products; all types of vegetables, especially fresh green vegetables; a little saturated and some polyunsaturated fat. If you do consider supplements over and above this healthy diet, a multi-vitamin and mineral capsule once a day should top up any deficiencies without risk of overdose or wasting money.

Q   **I've heard of hyperactive children, but what about me? I'm 47, my children don't need much attention nowadays, but I simply can't relax. I must always be up and doing.**

A   Many women get into a pattern of activity, worry, sleeplessness, worry about sleeplessness, and fatigue. It may be that too much was demanded of you when the children were younger; you felt too great a sense of responsibility for them and the running of the house and you were always working against time to get things done. Now that you do have more time to yourself, you just can't sit down for a bit with a good book and let the world pass by.

It's easy to tell someone to relax but most of us need to know *how*. It isn't just a question of taking a rest. As you probably know all too well, it's when you're 'resting' that a thousand-and-one pressing things that you think need to be done come to mind. Two things may help. First, ask yourself just what demands are really being made on you. Could you adjust your day so that you do the really important things but let the others look after themselves? Who says that every single item of clothing has to be ironed, every room dusted daily, every cup rinsed as soon as it's used? You will probably be able to think of other activities that force you to rush round busily, but which really aren't at all pressing.

The second thing is to learn a relaxation technique. This does not mean just sitting doing nothing; it means learning consciously to relax every muscle in your body, and the thoughts in your brain. It's difficult to do this by yourself, but there are 'relaxation tapes' available (ask in a large record shop), local relaxation classes, and an audio-cassette course available from Relaxation for Living* to help you. There are several different methods of achieving the same result, and the Relaxation for Living course guides you through each so that you can choose the one that's most effective for *you*. You must be prepared to set aside about 20 minutes a day if the tapes are to bring results. Whatever else they achieve, they will ensure that you have at least that time to yourself.

You should also make a point of having a regular outing or visit to people you like. Some women actually feel guilty about doing anything they enjoy, but going out to the cinema or theatre, or for a meal cooked by someone else, or taking a holiday (if you can afford it), are essential for everyone's mental health. You aren't being selfish if you get away from the family and enjoy yourself in your own way once a week.

**Q** **If I go to the doctor with any ailment he's not interested. He always says 'It's just your age'. Am I right not to accept that ill-health in my sixties is just part of life?**

**A** You're quite right not to accept that people past their first youth inevitably suffer all sorts of ills. While it's perfectly true that some conditions are more prevalent in older than in younger people, this doesn't necessarily mean that they're *caused* by old age. If you've read the answers to earlier questions in this chapter, you'll have seen that there's a great deal we can do, throughout our lives, to prevent the development of many of the so-called ills of old age. And even if, through lack of knowledge or other circumstances, we haven't been able to follow a healthy regime up to now, it's never too late to change. A simple example is the woman whose walking became increasingly restricted through pain in her hips and knees until she started joint-rotating exercises every day before she went out. After a few weeks all that remained of the joint pain was a little morning stiffness, which rapidly went as soon as she started to move around. A man who took seriously his diagnosis of mild Type II diabetes, changed his diet to cut out almost all sugar-containing foods, and walked to work instead of taking a bus, was discharged from the diabetic clinic two years later as no trace of sugar was found in his blood or urine. Both these people *could* have relied on medication, possibly with bad side-effects, to control their conditions, though less effectively.

When your doctor tells you that you just have to expect certain troubles now you're in your sixties, ask firstly, what evidence there is that this condition is a disease caused by old age; and secondly, what self-help steps could alleviate it, preferably without drugs. It may be that if your doctor continues to adopt this fatalistic attitude you would find more help from a practitioner of alternative medicine, such as an osteopath, chiropractor or acupuncturist. Just make sure, if you do decide to consult a non-medical person, that she or he is a member of a recognized body that insists on standards of competence and ethics. The last book on the list at the end of the chapter is a useful source of information and you should find it in the reference section of your public library. The Institute for Complementary Medicine* can supply information about natural treatments and people who practise them. The Women's Health Information Center,* in the US, answers letters or telephone calls for a small fee. The National Self-Help Clearinghouse* is an American information and referral centre.

## Further reading

*Arthritis* Professor Paul A. Dieppe (Family Doctor Guides BMA/Thorsons)

*The Directory of Holistic Medicine and Alternate Health Care Services in the USA* Shirley Linde and Donald Carrow (Health Plus Publishers, P.O. Box 22001, Phoenix, AZ 85028)

*Eating for Health* Christopher Robbins (Granada)

*Eating Well on a Budget* (Age Concern* Recipes for pensioners)

*Exercise for the Over Fifties* Russell Gibbs (Jill Norman)

*Exercise: Why Bother?* (Sports Council)

*Food for Thought* (Health Education Authority — Free from local health education units)

*The Handbook of Complementary Medicine* Stephen Fulder (Ed.) (Oxford)

*The High-Fibre Cookbook: Recipes for Good Health* Pamela Westland (Dunitz)

*The New E For Additives* Maurice Hanssen (Thorsons)
*Ourselves, Growing Older* Boston Women's Health Book
    Collective (Collins)
*Osteoporosis* (National Osteoporosis Society)
*The Residue Report: The Action Plan for Safer Food*
    Stephanie Lashford (Thorsons)

# 2   Emotional problems

**Q** My sister says I must really pull myself together. I just don't seem to be able to get anything done. I sit around all day and I just can't be bothered to look after the house.

**A** Feeling as you do, encouragement to 'pull yourself together' is useless. Obviously you would if you could. The problem is that you simply can't – without help.

The first thing to consider is your physical condition; your lack of vitality could have a medical cause, and that needs investigation. If you've recently suffered from illness or great emotional stress, this could be an important factor. For example, if things have gone wrong with your marriage, or in your relationships with your children or other relatives, or you're suffering from financial worries, bad housing, or the loss of friends, any one of these things could make you feel low and apathetic, when everything seems just too much trouble.

So, do go to your doctor. Ask the receptionist to give you an appointment at a time when she or he won't be too busy and explain just how you feel, and try to talk about anything you think may have caused this depression. Depending on the sort of doctor you have (some, unfortunately, will just hand out tranquillizers, which could make the situation worse) you should be given a simple physical check-up and some suggestions about counselling or a referral to a consultant. If your doctor thinks that the depression can be lifted by prescribed anti-depressants it may be worth taking them. Anti-depressants don't cure a depression that has clear social, situational causes, but they can tide you over until you're in a position to cope with them. They do help many people and, unlike tranquillizers, they're not addictive. But do ask about what is being prescribed, any likely side-effects, and what to do if, after about three weeks, you're not beginning to feel substantially better.

This tiredness and apathy are very common in people who are depressed, and once any physical cause has been ruled out, the support of a suitable counsellor to help you sort out your problems can be very helpful. Often a good friend's help and understanding are even better. Perhaps, in your case, you believe that your sister is too heavily involved in the family, or may be too unsympathetic, to fill this role. But if you can really get across to her that, try as you may, you simply can't do as she has suggested, and that this is a common condition, she may be the right person to give you the support you need. Your partner's understanding, too, is vital. Many men find it easier to detach themselves from what they see as emotional demands. But if a wife is depressed, it's her husband's problem as well as hers, and he should do everything possible to make things easier for her without nagging or criticizing. If you have teenage children, your husband's care and concern will help them, too, to understand what is going on, and provide a model for *their* behaviour.

All these measures will help you to see light at the end of the tunnel. Look after yourself: eat well, take exercise (a first-rate anti-depressant) even if you don't feel like it, undertake projects or go to entertainments you enjoy, and don't feel guilty about 'indulging' yourself. See all this as therapy – the quickest way to get you back to

normal, or at least to where you can cope with
your situation more effectively.

Q  **Why do I feel so depressed? I seem to have
everything anyone could want – a good
husband, a lovely home, grown-up children
who're doing well.**

A  Although some of the factors outlined in the
answer to the previous question are obvious
causes of depression, sometimes we feel depressed
for no apparent reason. Some research has shown
that there may be little-understood biochemical
factors at work, that's to say that some people's
brain chemistry makes them more liable to react
with depression to situations or events that don't
affect others in this way.

Then there's the comparatively recent
revelation that many more children than we used
to believe have been damaged or abused by adults.
In some cases they've suppressed what happened,
have grown up apparently well-adjusted, only to
fall prey to inexplicable bouts of depression later.
Marriage guidance counsellors are finding that
many of the clients who come to them with
relationship problems have such backgrounds,
even though the clients themselves have
'forgotten' about the incidents until counselling
enables them to recognize what happened in the
past and, if possible, come to terms with it. Even
though in your past there may be no such trauma,
most people accept that childhood relationships,
pressures and events shape the way an adult
thinks, feels and behaves. If your parents were
over-anxious about you, demanded impossibly
high standards, were cold and unloving, or didn't
seem to be much interested in you as a person,
any one of these factors can lead you to be
depressed about yourself now.

Despite what would appear to be a thoroughly
happy situation, you may have adopted standards

of achievement and behaviour that aren't realistic.
Women in particular seem prone to believe they
should be perfect – perfect wives, perfect
housewives, perfect mothers of perfect children,
perfect hostesses, perfect balancers of the
demands of work and home. Since not one of
these perfections is attainable on its own, let
alone in combination, someone with these
standards is bound to fail to live up to them.
Failure (real or imagined) is very depressing.

Whatever the other measures you take to
overcome your present depression, acceptance
that you're human, with human weaknesses and
foibles, that there's no one (except yourself)
breathing down your neck and imposing
unattainable standards on you, may help you to
relax and stop demanding so much of yourself.
You have many options. Re-think what you really
want out of life. Enjoy yourself in the way that's
best for you. Plan a relaxing or exciting holiday.
Make contact with old friends. Make time to
learn something new or take up an old activity.
Join an organization whose aims you support and
offer time or money to the cause. Feeling that
we're doing something useful for other people is
probably one of the best therapies of all. These
choices are yours.

**Q** **I get in a panic about everything. I can't even
invite good friends to dinner without getting
so anxious that I can't sleep for nights
beforehand. Then I panic about not sleeping.**

**A** A few years ago the answer for people suffering
such bouts of anxiety would have been
tranquillizers. Now that we know about their
horrible side-effects and addictive properties,
doctors normally prescribe them only for very
short periods to tide people over a real crisis such
as a bereavement. So we do now have to cope
with anxiety through our own resources, and with

the help of friends or professional counsellors.

You could ask yourself what it is about your lifestyle that makes you so anxious, and how you could modify it. Take the dinner party, for instance. There are several ways of coping with that. The first is to decide not to entertain formally for the present, but instead to invite your friends for afternoon tea, or after-dinner coffee, or Sunday morning pre-lunch drinks, all of which are far less demanding on the hostess than a full-scale dinner party (and often more enjoyable, anyway). The second solution is to simplify the occasion, so that your guests are given the sort of meal you produce for your family, with just double or three times the amount of food. Then you won't have to worry about complicated recipes, quantities, or any of the other planning details which keep you awake. Assuming that you give your family satisfying and tasty meals, your guests will appreciate them too. The third way of coping is simply to stop entertaining altogether. But this would really be a great pity when the other two options are available, and could make you become even more anxious if later you decide to ask people for a meal again.

A lot of women who get anxious about their responsibilities and worry that they may forget an item when shopping, or a vital ingredient in their recipe, or that the cake may collapse or the soufflé fail to rise, overcome their anxiety by making lists and being careful to follow a recipe step by step, even if it's a familiar one. For many of us a shopping list is vital. Others have to plan meals in advance, perhaps on a fortnightly schedule, accompanied by a basic shopping list that ensures that everything needed for a particular menu will be there when wanted. Some people keep a jotter always at the ready to note down anything they need to remember but might forget. It's amazing how these simple organizational steps can relieve those night-time anxieties and stop us lying awake pointlessly going over and over again something we need to do next day. Exactly the same system will work if your anxiety centres on the possibility of failure in your job. If you work in an office, before leaving every evening, write down what you need to do next day, and keep your desk diary meticulously filled with dates you need to remember.

Once something is on paper, most of us are able to forget about it until it's relevant. Developing a routine of this kind is always helpful, whether it's making sure you always leave your glasses in exactly the same place, switching on the answering machine as an invariable accompaniment to putting on a jacket to leave the house, checking the bank balance on a certain day of the month without fail etc.

Most of our anxiety, if we think about it, is concerned with fear of other people's opinion of us, or fear of failure to live up to our own standards. So what we need to do is re-think these standards and decide to learn to relax about ourselves and the impression we make on others. Some people are helped by the realization that *everyone* is affected to a greater or lesser extent by how they are perceived by other people: dressing fashionably is just one example of how we tend to change our behaviour to suit the current climate of behaviour and opinion, even though we might actually prefer an old style. We have a great need to conform. But as we get older and more mature it helps to consider just why we feel this need, and whether we couldn't perhaps take less notice of others' assessment of us and do our own thing. It's small-minded, surely, to look down on someone who doesn't follow the latest fashion, hasn't seen the latest film, doesn't know which knife to use. If we wouldn't react towards others in this way, why should we expect that other people would towards us? And are such small-minded people really worthy of our respect and emulation?

It may help if you can actually learn a
relaxation technique (see page 30) and practise it
regularly, and if you read a book such as the one
by Anne Dickson listed at the end of this chapter.
Once you've gained confidence in yourself, you
need no longer fear the (often imagined)
disapproval of other people, and the anxiety that
such fear generates will disappear.

If your 'panic' is really that, rather than just an
anxiety that you may not be able to cope, you
may need professional help. Your doctor is the
first person to consult should your life be badly
affected by (for example) inability to leave your
house, feelings of faintness in public places, fear
of cars, trains or planes. The doctor may be able
to refer you on to someone who can offer help – a
clinical psychologist, for example.

**Q** **Since we moved and my husband spends
longer travelling to and from work, I'm on my
own most of the day. My teenage children
breeze in after school but are too busy with
homework to talk to me.**

**A** Loneliness is a big problem for many women,
especially those uprooted from familiar
surroundings or forced by circumstances to live
alone after widowhood or divorce.

How do you spend your day? With teenage
children you probably don't need to give full-time
attention to running the house; but on the other
hand you still feel the need to be there when they
get home from school. The answer seems to be to
find something to absorb your interest and energy
during those middle-of-the-day hours, something
that involves being with people.

With the smaller number of younger people
leaving school nowadays, there will be an
increasing opportunity for mature women to fill
job vacancies, and employers will be forced to
change their attitudes to part-time working. Since

your priority will be to get out of the house and work alongside others, you may be willing for a start to take work that fulfils that need rather than makes full use of your former qualifications and skills. Once in work, you could find that your employer will recognize your abilities and different, more compatible work could come your way. Offices, shops, schools all have jobs suitable for part-timers. You could go through the usual agencies, answer local advertisements, or simply ask a potential employer about vacancies.

Although it would be nice to find some form of home-working to fill the empty hours (and for someone in an isolated area and without transport this may be the only option) that wouldn't be the whole answer. You need people around you.

The other possibility, of course, is voluntary work. You could find out about local organizations and groups – a public library is a good source – choose one whose aims appeal to you, and offer your services. Many political, environmental and charitable organizations welcome people able to devote a set number of hours a week, and women who help voluntary groups find that the companionship and the friendship that develop give them just as much out of membership as they give in time and commitment.

Don't neglect your neighbours, either. The woman next door or down the street may be feeling just as lonely as you are, and just as shy about making contact. It takes a bit of nerve to approach a stranger, and of course you do risk a rebuff. But contacts made over walking the dog, going to the same shop, even delivering a wrongly-addressed letter, can break the ice. Then an invitation to tea or a morning coffee – on the spot or with a definite day and time suggested – can lead to getting to know each other better. Of course, if you really don't have much in common the friendship may not develop, but it's always worth a try.

Adult education classes, parent-teacher associations and women's organizations such as the Townswomen's Guild,* the Women's Institute,* the Co-operative Women's Guild* and the National Women's Register* in the UK, and their sister organizations elsewhere, provide meeting places from which individual friendships develop.

**Q** **Now that my children have all left home and my husband has left me, I wonder what my life is all about. I seem to have served my turn.**

**A** Certainly you appear to have reached a turning-point in your life, but that implies that you have the option to choose a new road. No one would underestimate the difficulty you face in adjusting from a situation where you were probably the hub of the family to one in which no one seems really to need you any more. So many women devote themselves totally to the needs of husband and children that they have had no time to give to *themselves*.

We are brought up to believe that our chief role in life is to serve and nurture others. Inevitably the day must come when we aren't needed in that capacity as much as before – or even at all. That's why it's so important for younger women to look ahead to the time when they, too, will no longer be completely absorbed in family life. Not only should we be educating and training our daughters to make full use of their talents and abilities while they have no family respons-ibilities, but we should encourage them to maintain their interests and skills during the child-rearing years. Then the switch from domes-ticity to part-time work to full-time employment will be made easily, as the years go by.

At present you are suffering from the shock of finding yourself suddenly without a partner and without your children. Such a loss can make anyone very depressed. Read the questions and answers on pages 34 to 37 for suggestions about ways of coping with depression, and the answer to the question before this one for ways of overcoming loneliness.

Sad as you feel at the moment, try to accept that, for the first time in your life, you are free of responsibility for others, free to be your own person. You can come and go as you like, stay in bed all morning if you want to, watch the TV programmes *you* like, invite relatives and friends your family didn't much care for, skip meals occasionally in favour of a snack, do things on impulse rather than arrange them round the needs of the family. Many women have found completely new interests in middle age or their later years once they're released from domesticity. The positive side of the loneliness coin is *independence*.

At 40 or 50 or 60 you still have years of life before you, years which you can enjoy in maturity in a way you never could when you were younger. Given good health (and that's partly up to you) and a reasonable standard of living, you can contribute to the welfare and happiness of others and derive a great deal of satisfaction yourself. If we can stay up and doing well into old age, we'll keep physically fit and mentally alert, getting the most out of life right to the very end.

Q **Agony aunts always seem to tell lonely or depressed people to go to evening classes, or join voluntary agencies. I'm sure that's right, but what if, like me, you're so shy you can't take the first step?**

A Certainly this is a situation in which the first step is the most difficult. How many of us have dreaded going to a party where we knew few people, but have actually enjoyed ourselves once we've got there? We went, probably, because not going would have offended our hostess, or because our boss expected it of us. In other words, we couldn't refuse. Refusing would have caused more embarrassment than actually turning up.

In other words, we were motivated to take that first step over the threshold. We had to overcome our shyness or fear of people and social situations. And things turned out unexpectedly well!

You've probably been in exactly that, or a similar, situation. If you could get over your shyness then, you can do so again. Don't say to yourself that you'll take that first step some time, or after the holidays, or in the New Year. Grit your teeth if you have to, seize the first opportunity (or make one) and talk to your neighbour; telephone the secretary of the Residents' Association or sports club, and ask about meetings, activities and membership; ask at the library about that evening class you'd like to attend, and find out whether you can join. Not next week – now. And follow up. The first initiative must be yours.

The first step is over. Now comes the second. You know where the meeting is and what time it starts. Go. And the moment you get there make contact with the person you spoke to, or someone who seems to be organizing things; or, if she or he is not in evidence, talk to *anyone*. Explain that you're new to the scene and you'd appreciate it if she could tell you what's going to happen and what you can do. If the person you've chosen knows the ropes it's likely that she's overcome any shyness she might have had, and could be helpful to you. If she, too, happens to be a new member, then you can laugh about the blind leading the blind, and that too could be the start of a relationship.

Try to arrange with this new acquaintance that either you'll pick each other up to go the next meeting, or that you'll definitely see each other there next time. Exchange telephone numbers if that seems appropriate. Most people will meet friendliness with friendliness, but you do have to pick the right person. Don't break into an obvious group. Wait to find someone on her own like yourself, sit next to her and be willing to make the first remark. Good organizations are well aware of the difficulties experienced by newcomers, and are on the lookout for anyone who seems to be lost or isolated; some actually appoint someone to welcome any new members and put them at ease.

Yes, the first steps are the most difficult, but knowing *that* can encourage us to take them. Having done so, confidence can soar.

Shyness can be cured, but it does take some personal effort. You may never be the life and soul of the party (you may not want to be) but you can gain sufficient confidence to hold your own in any situation, make sensible conversation, and not be overawed and feel inadequate – which is what shyness is all about. It often helps a shy person to realize that everyone's in the same boat. The loud-mouthed exhibitionist may be choosing that way to cover up his fear or feelings of inadequacy.

Once you're absorbed in what is going on around you, the personality and interests of other people, you'll relax and positively enjoy the situation. It really is worth putting up with a little embarrassment to reach that goal.

# Further reading

*Dealing with Depression* Kathy Nairne and Gerrilyn Smith (Women's Press)

*Depression: The Way Out of Your Prison* Dorothy Rowe (Routledge & Kegan Paul)

*Finding Our Own Solutions – Women's Experience of Mental Health Care* Women in Mind (MIND*)

*In Our Own Hands: A Book of Self-help Therapy* Sheila Ernst and Lucy Goodison (Women's Press)

*A Woman in Your Own Right* Anne Dickson (Pan)

# 3   Sex and relationships

Q I'm approaching the menopause and the
children are off our hands. I'm always reading
about the sex lives of middle-aged and older
people. Surely once we've completed our
family sexual intercourse is unnecessary?

A For anyone who has always seen sexual
intercourse as a means to an end – the production
of children – it may seem logical to think that
once you can no longer reproduce, sex is
pointless. And there are women who say that part
of the pleasure they've had from sex has been
linked with the possibility of pregnancy, so that
when that possibility no longer operates, their
interest wanes.

But for most people, women and men, there's a
lot more to sex than producing babies. If that
were the only purpose of sex, we would enjoy
intercourse only at the time of the month when
we're fertile, just a few days in the middle of the
cycle. Clearly for most people that doesn't apply;
moreover, many post-menopausal women claim
that once pregnancy is no longer possible, they
enjoy sex more than ever before. Since anxiety
about unwanted pregnancy and the possible
failure of contraception are no longer present,
they can relax and get the most physical and
emotional pleasures out of the loving relationship
with their partner.

If your feelings about sex have always been that

it's an inescapable but not very pleasant duty, clearly it's difficult in your forties and fifties to change. You were probably brought up to think like that, and what your mother told you, and your grandmother's influence on *her*, are still very powerful influences on your feelings now. It is understandable that fear of sex and its possible consequences (a child born out of wedlock) was so overwhelming until recent times; society in general moralized about 'loose women' and those 'abnormal' enough actually to enjoy sex. Such women were perceived as a threat to an ordered family life and might be the cause of an ultimate break up of society, so they had to be condemned. Meanwhile, the 'pure' woman endured her husband's attentions, in the hope that by doing so she would prevent him straying elsewhere.

With the arrival of contraceptive methods which, although far from perfect, do greatly reduce the risk of pregnancy, a more accepting attitude towards single parenthood, and the availability, in certain circumstances, of abortion, we have been able to rethink our attitudes and change our behaviour. We have been able to divorce sex from reproduction, enjoy its physical manifestations and the closeness and love of which it's one expression, without fear or guilt.

Despite the lurid tales you may have read, it does seem that as we get older we no longer have the urgent need of sexual satisfaction that may have driven us in our teens and twenties. But this doesn't mean that sexual activity ceases altogether, nor that, when it happens, it need be any less pleasurable. With the family's demands (and presence) less obtrusive, more time for ourselves, perhaps more comfortable circumstances than ever before, we're more able to relax, take our time, learn more about the needs and preferences of our partner and ourselves. Although you are older, you're probably wiser, more willing to understand and accept other people and their personalities. In no way are you

'past it'. There could be a lot of pleasurable
feelings just waiting to be released.

**Q** **I've been married for many years and I have
to admit I'm bored with sex.**

**A** In any aspect of our lives, a rigid routine can be
stultifying and boring. And unfortunately, many
couples do develop routine sex over the years. If
you always follow the same sequence in
lovemaking, there's no element of surprise and
little excitement. If what used to turn you on no
longer does so, it could be that you and your
husband need to explore other ways of enjoying
sex together.

Perhaps you could rethink your attitudes to
non-penetrative sex. To many people it comes as a
revelation to find that there's intense pleasure to
be gained by stroking, fondling and kissing parts
of the body that are not involved with genital sex.
And each of you probably knows how to get
pleasure from masturbation: share that knowledge
and apply what you've learnt to get even more
pleasure from each other.

Many couples find that by reading some of the
books listed below they derive new ideas about
sex. Nothing that gives pleasure to both partners
should be seen as weird or abnormal; but if either
of you finds any practice painful or distasteful,
you should say so, and the other should be
expected to show understanding and sensitivity
and not pursue it.

**Q** **Is it true that men need sex more than
women? I love my partner, but he wants to
make love every night, and can't understand it
when I say I don't feel like it every time.**

**A** People – men *and* women – vary very much in the
strength and frequency of their need for sex. As

with so many other aspects of a relationship, the solution lies in communication. Talk about how you feel; explain that it isn't that you reject him, or have no great interest in sex. It's just that you're different, and that there must be ways of compromising so that you're both happy.

Like many people you probably get a great deal out of 'non-sexual' ways of expressing your feelings. Some women actually avoid these contacts, because they're afraid of arousing sexual feelings in their partners which they don't feel ready to satisfy. They worry that it's somehow abnormal for a man with a partner to release his tensions by masturbation, when in fact many men will say that doing so in the presence of the woman they love adds a lot to the satisfaction they experience.

Q **I think my husband must be under-sexed. We have intercourse only a few times a year. I need it more often.**

A Of course there are differences in individuals' needs for sex. There can be physical reasons why a person's sex drive is low, too. If your husband seems generally under the weather, and he hasn't had a check-up recently, you could suggest a visit to the doctor; but suggest that it might be in his interests in general, don't make him feel defensive about his lack of interest in sex.

More likely, though, are the effects of stress and fatigue. If he's a workaholic, all his energies may be devoted to his daytime activities, and he is too tense or too tired to make love when he's *not* working. That needs to be discussed. It may be that in his view stress is inescapable because of the situation at work, or his boss, or he may be working hard in order to get promotion. How do you feel about that? Would you rather he earned less money and less status, but were more relaxed, with more time for you and the family? Or do you really share his aspirations and hope that somehow by overworking now he will earn the right to an easier life later? You need to sort all this out in your own mind, remembering that overwork can lead to far worse trouble than lack of interest in sex.

There are other measures you can take, too. A holiday – preferably without the children – in a pleasant place with time to do nothing, or something totally different from everyday life, may give you both new perspectives. It may be that in a more relaxed atmosphere you'll find that your husband has worries that he hasn't expressed before, and which could have some bearing on his feelings and behaviour. Getting away from immediate pressures is often the best way of resolving conflicting demands. Whatever he tells you about himself in these circumstances, you will want to reassure him of your love and support, and your willingness to co-operate in working out together the difficulties that may have arisen between you.

**Q** **Ever since my husband has come back from a business trip abroad I can't get rid of the suspicion that he may have caught AIDS. I really want to believe he's been faithful to me, and I daren't raise the question with him.**

**A** First of all, people don't 'catch' AIDS. What happens is that in the fortunately still fairly rare circumstances where people have been exposed to HIV (Human Immunodeficiency Virus) infection, they may have contracted HIV, which can later develop into full-blown AIDS. If you have no reason to believe that your husband has exposed himself to this infection by having unprotected intercourse, using a shared needle for injecting drugs, or having a blood transfusion in a country where blood is not properly treated as it is in Britain, you should have no real cause for fear.

However, Department of Health literature and other books and leaflets listed below will give you much more information about HIV and AIDS, and this is something we all need. All the available information emphasizes that a couple, each of whom has had no other partner for many years, run no risk of developing HIV, unless they use shared needles with other drug takers.

If this worry isn't dispelled, and reading the literature doesn't help, then I think you owe it to your husband to voice your fears, which must be affecting your relationship. You can expect his reaction to be one of surprise, of course, but if he sees how worried you are, despite the fact that your anxiety seems to him quite unreasonable, perhaps he'll be willing to take a blood test. However, be warned: once someone has had a test for HIV this can go on to his medical record and, moreover, he may have to declare that he's had this test if he applies for life or private medical insurance in the future. So it's not something to be entered into lightly.

Your concern seems to spring from an insecurity about him and his relationship with you, and perhaps it's just as important to resolve that insecurity as your present anxiety about AIDS. It can poison your relationship with him if you feel you can't trust him. If talking about yourself and your feelings seems to lead nowhere, perhaps you need counselling. Your doctor can suggest a local counselling service; in the UK, Relate* (formerly the Marriage Guidance Council) has a lot of experience in helping couples with these difficulties.

**Q** **I've been divorced for several years. Recently I met a man with whom I have developed a good friendship. The next step would seem to be going to bed with him. But how can I really know he isn't HIV positive?**

**A** Unfortunately, you can't. A test for HIV (see above) can lead to some problems. The fact is that unless he has been completely celibate for many years, he could have picked up the infection through sexual intercourse with an infected woman, who herself could have been unaware that she was HIV positive. It's very important to understand that HIV and AIDS are now becoming possibilities for heterosexual people. In the US, AIDS in women who had become infected through heterosexual intercourse rose from 14 per cent of infected women in 1982 to about 30 per cent in 1988. In the UK the percentage of HIV-positive women who acquired the virus through heterosexual intercourse rose from 11 per cent in 1985 to about 40 per cent in 1988. There's every reason to believe that many more heterosexual women will be HIV positive now. Many of these women will have gone on to develop full-blown AIDS eventually. So, *women are at risk*.

If your friend understands how HIV can spread, he will know that there's just a possibility that he might unknowingly have become infected, and that he could pass this infection on to you. He will therefore quite understand your anxiety and decide that sex with a condom (safer sex) is a must. Of course it's difficult to suggest to anyone that he might have contracted the infection; but the more we know about HIV and AIDS the more we understand that almost anyone (except the totally celibate and people who have had only one 'faithful' partner for many years) could have been infected. This isn't scaremongering. Until a means of combating the illness is developed, and this still seems some time away, people who believe that it can't happen to them are taking a risk.

**Q** **How often should we have sex?**

**A** There's no *should* about it. Individuals' needs vary greatly, and averages don't mean much. It is usual for people forming new partnerships to have sex more frequently than those who have been in a stable relationship for many years, but of course there are many exceptions to this. So there are some couples making love many times a week, others once a month and others in between.

The happiest situation is when each partner's needs and wishes coincide with the other's, and sex can be a spontaneous expression of their feelings for each other. But if one partner feels less urgency of need, he or she doesn't deserve blame; feelings should be respected, and a compromise sought. It doesn't mean that the less eager partner is any the less loving, just that he or she expresses that love in a different form. Many people are deeply satisfied by holding, cuddling, stroking and the spontaneous hug or kiss. It doesn't have to be bed or nothing.

**Q** **Since my husband died I seem to have read more about men's sexual needs and I feel guilty that I didn't understand him. He may have believed that I was cold towards him.**

**A** The death of a partner often leaves the survivor with feelings of guilt. 'Why didn't I do or say this or that?' they may ask themselves.

From other answers to questions posed in this chapter you may have realized that people's (women's and men's) sex drives can vary very much and, despite all the myths, it isn't true that all men want sex at all hours of the day and night. As we've seen, if the couple can communicate with each other and if each is willing to 'pleasure' the other in the way that suits them best, the needs of both can be satisfied.

It is only in recent years that it has been possible to discuss in print the ways in which we can get sexual pleasure without penetration. Women and men have always masturbated, but this was kept as a guilty secret, and the idea that a married woman or man would do so was regarded as abnormal, if not downright wicked. It takes some time to dispel such misinformation, and the result has been that many older couples have been too embarrassed to talk about their real needs with their partner. They may know what turns them on and leads to orgasm, but they can't bring themselves to tell the partner what this is. We now know, for instance, that for most women orgasm is reached by stimulation of the clitoris, with or without the male penis entering the vagina. Because this wasn't openly talked about, very many women have seldom, or never, reached a climax and it isn't surprising that sex has been unsatisfying for them.

If your and your husband's sexual activity was not very enjoyable for you, you probably didn't seek it, or make the first move. If now you believe that your husband interpreted this as rejection of him, you shouldn't feel guilty about it. It was ignorance on his part as much as on yours that resulted in your lack of interest in sex. Perhaps sex for you meant nothing more than quick penetration and orgasm for your husband, leaving you unsatisfied and actually trying to avoid this situation. With hindsight, and with the knowledge you have acquired, you may now see that this was unfortunate – but you can't blame yourself.

Q **How can I explain my sexual needs to my partner?**

A Sex manuals used to make much of 'foreplay' without really explaining what this was. Certainly it involves close bodily contact, and stroking and kissing those parts of the body that respond to this stimulation. But it also involves manual or oral stimulation of the genitals – in women, specifically the clitoris. Far from being 'foreplay' (something that happens before the real business of sexual intercourse) for many women this is what brings orgasm: sometimes while their partner's penis has entered the vagina, sometimes before and sometimes after he has reached his climax.

You probably know through having practised masturbation how to reach orgasm, and your partner knows this about himself, too. By words or actions you can show each other just what is right for you. These are not secrets to be kept from each other, but something that will add greatly to your sexual fulfilment.

**Q** **Although I'm quite convinced that he's never had an affair I keep worrying that my husband is surrounded by younger women at work. How can I compete?**

**A** Nothing is more counterproductive than jealousy and suspicion. A stable, long-term relationship has so much going for it, and you have every reason to believe that your husband has been faithful. You've undoubtedly weathered a lot of storms together; you've brought up a family; made a home; established links with family, friends and your neighbourhood. What can your husband's young colleagues offer to compare with all that? Certainly some men are flattered by the attentions of a young woman, and may even consider forming a relationship with one of them. But nine times out of ten this is not a permanent one, and a man whose wife and family mean much to him resists the temptation to get embroiled in something that would be so threatening to the marriage, as *you* would, if the boot were on the other foot.

Unless you have strong evidence that your
husband's mild interest in these young women is
developing into something more than just that, it
would be best to accept it for what it is. Trust
between married people is important, and it can
be jeopardized if either of them behaves with
unreasonable suspicion towards the partner. The
fact that your husband talks to you about his
colleagues would seem to indicate that he has
nothing to feel guilty about.

Q  **My husband has been consistently unfaithful
ever since our marriage fifteen years ago.
Every time I find out about an affair he says
he can't help it, and he has concealed the
situation because he doesn't want to hurt me.
But I *am* hurt. I feel like a battered wife,
without the bruises to show for it. He says he
loves me and wouldn't leave me for any of
these girls. And I can't afford to leave him.
Who's at fault – him or me?**

A  No single piece of advice will solve this problem.
There's such a long history behind your husband's
unfaithfulness, and your reaction to it, which
would need unravelling in a face-to-face situation.
I think you may be wrong in trying to
apportion blame. On the face of it, you've had a
lot to put up with, and it seems that it's only now
that you are letting things get you down. It also
seems that you are unwilling or unable to issue
him with an ultimatum; and the fact that you
have accepted his affairs over the years, when he
tells you he can't help himself, has enabled him,
to put it bluntly, to have his cake and eat it.
Perhaps you've now reached the limit of tolerance.
Perhaps if he were really faced with a choice he
would not persist in these affairs, which he knows
have such an effect on you and could lead to the
ultimate break-up of the marriage. If he really

means what he says, how would he react to your saying, and meaning, that if he doesn't end his present affair, and reject any other potential ones, you'll get a divorce? It's probably true when he says he loves you and needs you. But it seems that he will only change his ways, and grow up, if he really believes that he just can't go on in this immature way and still retain love and respect.

Of course it's extremely difficult to stand firm and determinedly carry out a threat of this kind. That's why you really need outside help. You need to believe in yourself, to reject any idea that you're abnormal in not being able to accept the pain and humiliation he's inflicting on you. If he cares for you as he claims he does, he must be made to see that no-one could accept what he is doing to you. Perhaps counselling could give you the strength to carry through what you now believe you need to do, and help you towards independence.

You're still quite young. Your future shouldn't be overshadowed by the misery and depression you're experiencing. There's no magic formula – the way ahead could be very hard. But wouldn't it be better than what you're going through at present? Of course it's possible that a severe shake-up would make your husband realize how much you really mean to him, and to make a choice: to repair the damage or face the consequences. It seems he's never had to face such a stark choice before.

But it would be sensible to prepare yourself for the possibility that the marriage can't be saved. This is where counselling could provide you with some emotional support. A good counsellor would help you to understand how you really feel and enable you to make your own decisions. She wouldn't tell you what to do – no one can do that. What counselling can do is to help you sort out your feelings and take appropriate action.

Relate* (formerly the Marriage Guidance Council) is the organization to contact. They're listed in the telephone directory, or you can get the address of a local branch from their head office.

**Q** **I'm single after the break-up of a relationship some years ago. I'm getting older-looking all the time. Who would want me now?**

**A** It's really tragic how much we conform to society's belief that the only woman attractive enough to 'catch a man' is young and pretty. We've been brainwashed by the male-dominated advertising industry and the media generally with this insidious idea, and we see the incredible difference in attitudes to ageing men and women when a middle-aged female TV presenter gets sacked, or shifted to something less visible, while wrinkles, grey hair and being overweight seem no barrier to media success for men.

We really need to rethink our attitudes and values. A vigorous, healthy, outgoing woman of any age is always attractive to others. She doesn't have to conform to some fantasy stereotype of youth and sexiness. She'll have friends of all ages, and most of them will forget what her chronological age is in the pleasure of contact with her.

If we rely on these stereotypes of what constitutes sexual attraction, and believe that it's so important, of course we're going to feel inferior and unwanted as we get older. And if we rely for our happiness solely on a relationship with a man, whether or not he's really compatible, we'll be a great deal less happy than we would be leading independent self-reliant lives. It's interesting that many years ago research found that the group suffering least from depression was single women. Married women suffered nearly as much depression as unmarried men, who came top of this unenviable league. There must be a lesson here.

The days when a single woman was looked upon as a failure are long gone. She's likely to be good at her job, well-respected in the community and – yes – even envied by those of her friends who are hanging on to an unsatisfactory relationship for the sake of their personal security and the needs of their children. Unlike them, she's had no career-break to cope with; she has the freedom to come and go as she pleases without the pressure to conform to others' demands. She may believe she's missed out by not having had children; but as any mother will tell you, she'll have missed out on some worry and heartache too. As long as you retain your interest in other people and the world around you, enjoy the benefits of friendship and the equal pleasures of being alone, you won't take to heart the physical toll of the years.

# Further reading

*AIDS and You* (Health Education Authority) Free from local health education units
*Enjoy Sex in the Middle Years* Christine Sandford (Optima)
*Woman's Experience of Sex* Sheila Kitzinger (Penguin)
*Women and the AIDS Crisis* Diane Richardson (Pandora)
*Women and Sex* Anne Hooper (Sheldon Press)

# 4 Starting again

**Q** **I've just been through a painful divorce. I feel lost and bewildered. How can I regain my confidence?**

**A** No one can go through the experience of loss and come out unscathed. You've lost a lot – love, security and past hopes – however sensible a step that divorce seemed to be. If the process of divorce was particularly damaging, you may have even more to put up with. It's no wonder you feel so upset now, and so unsure of yourself and your future. Healing after such an experience does take time.

That's the most important thing to realize. Accept that your feelings are likely to be raw and your equilibrium badly affected for the present, and therefore that you're particularly vulnerable to making bad decisions. You'd be wise to make as few important ones as possible.

Some women in this situation rush into new relationships, as an antidote to the loss of self-respect that results from their divorce. Others keep busy by moving house, changing jobs, spending money they can't afford – anything to take their mind off what has happened. When we're low and depressed (as you seem to be) our judgement is impaired, and it's all too easy to make foolish mistakes and take inappropriate decisions which we later regret. Thus we lay up even more trouble for ourselves, trouble it may be even more difficult to get out of than carrying through the decision to get a divorce.

So it would be wise to try, as far as you can, to coast along while you gradually sort out your emotions and your way of life. Now may be the time to renew old friendships which may have suffered during your stormy marriage; to return to activities you used to enjoy; to offer help to people who need it, whether through personal contact or through a voluntary organization. If you're in a job that keeps you busy, stick with it, because there's nothing like having real work to do to keep the mind actively occupied, and so temporarily forget troubles. If you find being alone difficult to bear, train yourself gradually to accept that there are pleasures to be gained in solitude. Don't fill every spare moment with frantic activity. Spend some time each week at home by yourself as well as with family and friends.

Gradually you'll feel more able to cope with whatever life now offers you, more confident about yourself. And *that's* the time to make real changes, if they seem appropriate. Consider changing jobs or trying for promotion; working for a further qualification; moving house; arranging to go on holiday with a friend; joining a women's group or a political party. While you needn't rule out the possibility of a new intimate relationship, try to accept that it may never happen, and that if it does, it will develop slowly and naturally from the contacts and activities of your daily life. You may feel so devastated by the experience you've recently been through that you're determined it will never happen again. That will make you sensibly wary, but it needn't close your mind.

Learn to believe in yourself. Everyone has something to offer – some ability, talent, life experience. Don't be hard on yourself; like everyone else you have a right to develop your interests and enjoy yourself. You may feel now that life will never be the same again – and of course that's true. But it could be better.

**Q** **I feel quite persecuted by my family and friends. They all say that I ought to marry again, to give the children a father. Life as a single parent is hard, but surely it's better than rushing into what might be an unsatisfactory marriage?**

**A** You're quite right not to rush into anything. And you're just as right to resist the pressure to remarry, however well meant, for the sake of anybody, even your children. It's amazing how a widowed or divorced woman is bombarded by unwanted advice about how she should run her life. It's sad that people can't accept that decisions about how we should live must be ours alone. Even if we ask our friends for advice, we don't have to take it.

Make sure you're getting all the financial support you're entitled to, either from social security or from your ex-husband. If your friends are anxious to help, enlist them for outings with the children, or as baby-sitters, to enable you to get out regularly. Your father or brother can provide your boys with the male company you may think they need. Many single-parent families manage very well, despite some material hardships, and it's been proved time and again that children with a secure home background can be more stable and adjusted than those whose parents have stuck together 'for the children's sake' in the midst of rows and bitterness.

**Q** **My brother's wife died a year ago. He just seems unable to get over it. He's helpless about everything and relies on me to look after his house, give him regular meals and so on. I feel it's time for him to help himself.**

**A** It's generally recognized that it takes time – at least two years – for many people to start leading

normal (if changed) lives after the loss of a
partner. But this doesn't happen suddenly:
adjustment develops over time, and after a year it
would seem that your brother should be
beginning to take more responsibility for himself.
He may still need you for some material and
emotional support, but not to run his life for him.

His apathy and inability to take initiatives
himself show that he's still very depressed, so I
think that one thing you could do for him is to
suggest that he sees his doctor. Although no
doctor and no medicine can repair his loss, and he
will have to come to terms with it eventually, it's
possible that therapy and/or medication could see
him over his present mood and enable him to
take a more balanced and active part in running
his life.

Then you could suggest to him that he comes
to you once or twice a week for a meal, but that
you'll show him how to fend for himself in the
kitchen so that he's mostly independent of you.
There are simple basic cook books, and some
ready-made meals are nutritious and very easy to
prepare (though of course fresh food is better, and
he should gradually learn to use it). Many men
have no idea of food preparation and cooking, still
less of nutrition. But once they're interested, they
can become quite scientific about planning meals
and even get some enjoyment out of doing so. It's
a pity that there are still women who actively
discourage this sort of interest and ability, leaving
their men helpless in emergencies or if forced to
live alone.

The same technique could be applied to
housework. You and your brother may not aim for
perfection, but he could be taught how to use
household appliances and keep the place
reasonably tidy and clean. Your need to oversee
his housework should decrease until he's able to
undertake it all himself.

Of course you understand how bereft he feels
and you sympathize with his grief. But the

kindest thing you can do now is to encourage him
to live independently. Don't let him see your
advice as rejection – it isn't that. A gradual
withdrawal of your everyday support, though, is in
his best interests as well as yours.

Q My marriage was a very happy one. My
husband died two years ago, but I still feel
shattered. How can I ever be happy again?

A Once it has ended through death or separation, a
good relationship can never be exactly replaced.
You are still grieving over your very sad loss, and
no one would expect to see you behaving as
though it hadn't happened. Perhaps you have been
too eager not to show that grief and have put a
brave face on things with family and friends. But
of course the hurt is still there.

You probably still feel the need to talk about
your husband to people who knew him. There
must be people around you who would be glad to
share memories in this way, and to help you in
any way they can to adjust to a different kind of
life. It is often difficult for others to know just
how they can help. They're anxious to do so, but
wait to be asked rather than risk upsetting the
bereaved person by talking about the loss, which
they believe she may be unwilling to do. So you
may have to take the first step with one of your
close friends, telling her how you feel and what
the bereavement has done to you. By
remembering the happy times and everything that
your husband meant to you, you can come closer
to acceptance of what has happened, and
gradually start to rebuild your life.

In friendship, in work, in contact with children
or grandchildren you will find a new kind of
satisfaction. True, there is no substitute for a
close and loving relationship with a life-partner,
but circumstances can provide another kind of
contentment, if we let them.

Q After a few years of marriage I found that my husband bore no resemblance to the man I thought I loved. He kept me short of money, rejected our children and was often away from home without explanation. Eventually I discovered he'd been leading a double life. His friends all knew about it – I didn't. Now I'm divorced. How can I ever trust a man again?

A The discovery must have been extremely painful to you, especially as you feel so humiliated that you were the last person to know what was going on. You have every right to feel cheated and disillusioned.

You probably *will* find it difficult to give your trust again. You'll feel that if you've been cheated once, you could be conned again. But that would be to accept that you haven't learnt anything from your experience – and clearly you have.

Naturally you'll be wary about forming any new relationship and committing yourself in any way. That would be sensible. So many people ignore and don't want to recognize the many small signs that a new acquaintance may put out to show that she or he may be untrustworthy or basically incompatible. If a person is dishonest in his dealings with you or anyone else, no matter how trivial the occasion, that should produce a warning light. If he's irritable and moody, you may think it's just a passing phase. But couldn't it be part of his nature which could get worse instead of better the longer he knows you? A person who drinks too much, drives recklessly, slags off friends, boasts of past conquests or is constantly telling stories whose aim is self-aggrandizement is unlikely to drop these unpleasant forms of behaviour, or versions of them, in a new relationship.

Many men are violent; many women are devious. But this doesn't mean that every man is a potential murderer or that every woman will

manoeuvre against you behind your back. We all
have to exercise our judgement about people in
the light of our experiences, and not allow
ourselves to overlook warning signs, or to believe
that we have it in our power to change a person's
character. If we adopt this attitude, we can move
slowly towards intimacy as we become more and
more aware of positive signs that an individual is
someone we can really trust. And that applies to
friends of both sexes.

**Q** **People tell me I should have no problems
meeting new men. I lived with someone for
some time, but we split up on my initiative.
I'd like a friendship that might lead to
something deeper, but I wouldn't want to
commit myself too soon.**

**A** Most friendships are formed through work or the
sort of activity that absorbs a high proportion of
our time. Few lasting ones result from deliberate
attempts to meet a new partner, without the
backing of a common interest.

If your working life brings you into contact
with people, that should be enough to enable you
to take the first steps towards something more
than mere acquaintanceship. A drink or a meal
after work with a few colleagues (women and
men) at your suggestion; a cinema or theatre visit;
inviting some neighbours to a small party;
chatting to someone who seems isolated at a
social gathering or a political meeting: all these
are ways in which friendships can be formed, not
necessarily with the man of your dreams but with
his workmate or his sister.

Without being pushy, you do have to take
initiatives. You have to be prepared to follow them
up, too. And you must expect that, on better
acquaintance, you may decide that there's no
basis for a real friendship with a colleague or
client or fellow-member of your evening class.

That's just the luck of the draw – and no harm done.

The wider your circle of friends, the greater the likelihood of meeting someone with whom you have a lot in common. But in order to maintain a friendship network we do have to be willing to initiate contacts, it's so easy to let things drift and wait for someone else to make the first approach.

**Q** **I live alone and like it. Am I abnormal?**

**A** People's social needs vary as much as other human characteristics. To some it's very satisfying to shut the door on the world and do their own thing without needing to adjust to someone else's requirements. Others would get bored or intensely lonely without the comings-and-goings and chat of close companions.

As long as you don't barricade yourself in, emerging only for the bare necessities of life and never speaking to anyone at all, you're not abnormal. However, if your need to be alone results in self-neglect or a real terror of other people, you may need help and you should contact your doctor or a counselling agency.

**Q** **I've always got on better with women than with men, and now I realize that in fact I'm sexually attracted to a woman I've met through my job. This has devastated me. What can I do?**

**A** It's estimated that at least ten per cent of people are gay or lesbian. We don't really know how many more may be attracted to their own sex without actually practising homosexuality. So the first thing to realize is that you are not alone.

In the past people attracted to their own sex were seen as sick or disordered, and attempts were made to 'treat' them by medical or psychological means with the idea of a 'cure'. Nowadays it is recognized that this sizeable proportion of the population has equal rights with everyone else, and that they have neither the need nor the desire to change their sexual orientation.

Naturally if your whole background is such that you've been brought up to share outmoded attitudes to homosexuality, it's been a shock to discover the strength and nature of your feelings towards another woman. Whether or not your feelings are reciprocated, it will take time to accept them, and there may be some painful experiences in 'coming out' to your family. So you do need help.

Lesbian Line* in the UK can give you the number of a local counselling group where you can talk to a sympathetic person who'll accept you as you are, help you to come to terms with your feelings and anxieties, and tell you about publications, groups and organizations. The Older Lesbians' Network,* which can offer you ongoing support and information, meets regularly in London. Among organizations in the USA are Senior Action for a Gay Environment,* the Federation of Parents and Friends of Lesbians and Gays Inc,* and of course the Older Women's League.* Elsewhere women's liberation and feminist groups provide addresses of similar organizations.

**Q** **I feel foolish to say it, but I need a man! Yet I can never settle down in a partnership; things always go wrong. Is it better to feel sexually frustrated than to try to make a go of it with someone I actually don't really like?**

A This is the painful choice that many people have to make. Trial and error tend to convince some women that, whether they're too choosy and demand too high standards from a partner, or there just aren't any men around with whom they are going to be able to build a satisfying relationship, finding a possible partner will never happen.

If you think that your standards are so demanding that nothing but perfection in a partner will do, it's probably true that you will never be satisfied because, as the saying goes, no-one is perfect. If you're unwilling or unable to accept others' foibles and imperfections, sexual frustration may be the lesser evil than trying to adjust. This isn't to say that you should be willing to accept clear incompatibility, aggressive behaviour, neglect, or dishonesty in the hope that somehow a relationship with you would reform a flawed character; but to be realistic, most of us have to develop a degree of acceptance and tolerance if we're to find and maintain a good relationship.

Some people have to accept that in the end perhaps they really will never find someone with whom they could spend the rest of their days. The fact that single, independent women are no longer seen as failures, but may sometimes be actually envied for their ability to build their lives alone, makes this easier. And there are many middle-aged or older women who quite unexpectedly have found a partner whose outlook, lifestyle and sexual needs meet their own – once they have decided to stop looking!

Sexual frustration can be hard to bear. As with many other kinds of frustration, though, a solution can often be found in non-sexual friendships, satisfying work, and the development of wide and absorbing interests. Compared with a relationship that feels wrong from the start, and may only go from bad to worse, these are compensations that for most people far outweigh the lack of a regular sexual partner.

Q **I really like a man who works in the same office. I know he feels the same about me. We've begun to see a lot of each other after work, but there's nothing sexual in it. Is it really possible to be 'just friends'?**

A It will be a great step forward in human relations when women and men can get pleasure from one another's company in the same way as they can with members of the same sex.

Your problems may arise not from anything in the friendship itself, but in other people's perception of it. Gossip and insinuations might make things difficult for you in the office. And if either of you is married or in another relationship, a partner may need a lot of convincing that this is just a friendship, not a liaison.

You may be quite certain that no-one else is being harmed by your friendship, but you may have to face the fact that you could be forced to decide between continuing it and seriously upsetting a third person, or sacrificing it to protect an existing partnership. Just as you are doubtful about the possibility of a woman and a man remaining 'just friends', so a husband or wife may be convinced that there must be much more to your friendship than you're willing to admit. Suspicion and jealousy, however ill-founded, can poison a marriage. Ideally we should be able to accept that friendship can blossom between members of the opposite sex who have a lot in common. Realistically, most of us have to accept that possessiveness and sexual jealousy dominate human relationships as much today as they did in more primitive societies.

Most women are sceptical about 'open marriage', seeing it as a chiefly male excuse for indulging in extra-marital sex and salving the conscience by encouraging the partner to do likewise. A minority of couples seem to make the idea work, finding not only a variety of sexual experience but good friendships outside the marriage. Your relationship with your friend may never become a sexual one, but as there is some doubt in your mind, perhaps you should be prepared to face this situation if it arises. Better still, if you really don't want things to develop in that direction, you should be putting out signals to that effect, so that painful scenes of rejection and hurt feelings don't ever arise.

**Q** **Am I likely to meet a suitable marriage partner through a marriage bureau or dating agency?**

**A** If you are over 50, your chances of meeting a suitable partner are not at all good. Most reputable agencies won't put you on their books if there really is no likelihood of being able to find you a partner.

Younger women may be given a better choice. But make sure that the bureau you select is a member of the Association of British Introduction Agencies* (organizations that subscribe to an agreed Code of Practice).

Don't agree to meet anyone contacted through an agency at his home, or at yours, without another person present. It's best to meet in a public place such as a restaurant or pub. And do remember all the warnings about casual contacts and HIV infection and AIDS (see page 52).

**Q** **I'm considering remarriage, to an old friend. I think we could have a good future together as we have so much in common, but there isn't any sexual attraction about it on either side. Isn't love more important than sex?**

**A** Most happily married couples would agree with this proposition. Sex isn't *unimportant*, for most people, but a trusting, loving companionship means even more. Most youthful relationships are based at the beginning on sexual attraction, but without a developing pleasure in being together as people, they probably won't last.

Individuals differ in their needs and priorities. Despite the current tendency to encourage middle-aged and older people to believe that they should be as sexually active as they were in their youth, it seems to be a fact that for a majority sex, while still a part of the relationship, isn't as important as it used to be. No one need feel inadequate or strange because he or she rates a loving partnership more highly than sexual attraction. In considering marriage, though, it's as well to establish that both partners have the same attitudes. A frank discussion of priorities, beliefs and needs could save damaging confrontations later.

If we look around at our friends who have stayed together over the years, we'll see just how important to them common beliefs and an easy, accepting, loving relationship have been. We probably don't know how important a part sex has played in their lives – that's nobody's business but theirs – but what we can see, and perhaps envy, is their ability to live together as true friends as well as lovers.

Q **I'm 50 and my friend is 54. He's a widower; I've never been married. I'm naturally apprehensive about how our proposed marriage will work out.**

A A new relationship at any age requires adjustments, and even some compromises. You have probably got quite used to seeing yourself as a single woman; you've come to terms with the advantages and have perhaps accepted that the disadvantages are less important. He has had years of marriage, happy or unhappy, and must be just as anxious about the future with a new partner.

Part of your worry may stem from your past sexual experience, or perhaps the lack of it. Some of the books listed on page 59 may help you if you aren't too confident about how you're likely to react and what will be expected of you. If you're really inexperienced, do be willing to tell your fiancé so; there is nothing to be ashamed of, and it will help him if he realizes that things may develop more slowly between you than they would if you were sexually experienced. On the other hand, you may have had lovers in the past and that, too, needs to be talked about, your feelings about it clarified, and the past then laid to rest.

Marriage to someone who has been married before may involve something many women fear and dislike, which is moving into the house formerly occupied by the first wife. Often it's quite impractical to suggest a move away and a completely fresh start. But an understanding man will see that it's very difficult for a new wife to move into a house whose furnishings and equipment are just the same as they were before, and will be glad to refurnish where possible, change things round and redecorate to his bride's taste. More difficult may be the relationship with his children (see page 91), with his former in-laws, and his own family. Depending on what these relationships have involved, some suspicion and hostility may have to be faced; alternatively, their relative's new wife may be welcomed with acceptance or relief. That's another aspect that should be talked over in advance. Again, an understanding and mature man will be able to anticipate any difficulties and help his wife to overcome them.

Perhaps you're worried that you may have become set in your ways. It's very easy to develop personal routines and not to accept that other people have other ways of doing things. If you've ever shared accommodation with a friend you'll know how maddening unpunctuality, different kitchen routines, different ideas of hygiene, and little habits of untidiness or fussiness can be. Adjustments simply have to be made if small bickerings aren't to develop into major rows. Standards may have to be raised or dropped and a blind eye turned to unimportant differences of habit and behaviour. Each will care for the other regardless of whether she or he conforms to a rigid timetable or leaves lights on unnecessarily.

Part of the answer to the previous question may be useful to you as you look forward to this new stage in your life.

## Further reading

*Divorce: Legal Procedures and Financial Facts* (Consumers Association)

*Intimate Strangers* Robert Morley (Family Welfare Association)

*On Your Own: A Practical Guide to Independent Living* Jean Shapiro (Pandora)

*Women of a Certain Age: The Midlife Search for Self* Lillian B. Rubin (Harper & Row)

# 5   Grown-up children

Q   **My relationship with my daughter has always been very close. We depend on each other a lot. Now she's going to work hundreds of miles away. I just wonder how she'll get on without seeing me every day.**

A   Separation from people we love is often very painful. But your daughter is old enough to take a job away from home, and must therefore be old enough to live independently. No doubt she'll miss you and, if she's been dependent on you not only for material help but for emotional support too, she may find adjusting to her new life as difficult as you suspect. However, managing one's life on one's own is an essential part of growing up, and most people have to learn through making mistakes, without having them corrected or cushioned by a parent. Although at first you may find that she consults you at every turn, gradually she will realize that she may have relied too much upon you. Then she will see to it that she starts to make her own decisions, telling you about them perhaps, but basically going her own way. This is something to be welcomed.

'Letting go' of a child who for years has been genuinely and necessarily dependent on her parent is never easy. 'Mum knows best' may have applied in early childhood, but growing up involves growing away from a parent, however loving the relationship. If the relationship is good, there will be a continuing involvement and interest in each other's lives. Advice may be sought, but it needn't be followed. And advice unasked for can be greatly resented – it smacks of the *control* that every adolescent and young adult rightly rejects.

Having your daughter at some distance should make it easier for you to relax and let her lead her life in the way she wants than it would be if you had her with you on a daily basis.

You are concentrating on the difficulty *she* may have in adjusting to living so far away. It seems that the major difficulty is really yours. It will be up to you to judge each new situation as it arises, standing back most of the time, but being ready with help if your daughter seeks it. Even then, for her sake you may sometimes have to say 'no' or offer less than you would like to give, knowing that the bond of dependence has to be broken.

There are many parents of adult children who feel that the relationship has been really successful if parents and children lead their separate lives as loving friends who offer mutual support in times of trouble and share the pleasures of success and achievement. It's in your own interests as well as those of your daughter that you should now start to organize your life in such a way that she isn't the centre of it: work, friendships, caring for others in a wider circle, will all help to make *you* independent, too – a person in your own right.

Q My husband is such a 'manager', he can be quite overbearing with our son. He even tries to intervene when the boy has an interview for a job, offering unwanted advice, going along to 'give him moral support' by waiting outside. It can't be good for the boy.

A Parents who behave like this always believe that their motivation is to help. They don't see that these attempts at control demonstrate a lack of confidence and respect. In the event that this interference seems warranted, because the young person is so gauche or inept that he can't manage anything on his own, that must surely be a reflection not on him, but on his parent. If he's always been dominated and prevented from making his own decisions he may well be unable to do so in a new situation.

Sometimes a father or mother who behaves like this is trying to compensate for what they feel are their own failures and inadequacies. They'll go to enormous and quite inappropriate lengths to advise, protect and manage their son or daughter. In the end, of course, the child either breaks out or breaks down.

Your role, a very difficult one, will now be to take your turn at protection: not protection of your son against the outside world, but against the destructive power your husband tries to exercise. It may be that he uses the same pressure and tactics with you; if so, your example in resisting them will help your son. It may be difficult to discuss with your husband the stultifying and demeaning results that can stem from his behaviour, but if you can do so in a calm manner, using reason rather than emotional appeals, he may listen. You can do this by understanding that his motives are good, even if misguided; that there is something in him that demands satisfaction from the idea that he can make things right for his son, even if he hasn't been able to do so for himself; that his life experience is such that he has been thrown in some way into a 'managerial' stance and that he can't let this go, even within the family.

At the same time you can do everything to build up the young man's confidence in himself. Ask his opinion; suggest ways he can act independently and thus gain experience of thinking and doing for himself; give him as many opportunities as you can to behave like a proper

grown-up person. And you can encourage any
plans he may have to move away from home,
branch out independently, follow the kind of
career that suits him, and not necessarily his
father's or your own plans for him. Welcome his
friends and encourage contact with them, perhaps
ending a tradition of family holidays so that he
can go away with people of his own age. All this
will bring him closer to you in a positive way:
and it's just possible that when his father sees
that his son can make a success of things on his
own, he'll be more willing to let go with
confidence.

Q **I'm always busy. I have a fascinating job and
it really absorbs much of my interest and
energy. I just wonder whether this has made
me too remote from my teenage and older
children.**

A If you have no evidence that your job and lifestyle
have caused distress or disadvantage to the family,
your worries seem to be purely theoretical. There
are many young people who would be only too
glad to change places with your children, subject
as they are to possessive or domineering parents!

Many parents with absorbing jobs have
extremely warm and friendly relationships with
their children precisely because their lives aren't
totally centred on home and family. It isn't that
they don't care about their children, but that
they've been able to care enough to let them grow
up as self-reliant and independent people, while
living independent lives themselves.

Most working parents go to great lengths to see
that their younger children are properly cared for,
despite the inadequacy of childcare provision
(particularly in the UK) and the expense involved
in providing substitute care. Some research has
shown that relationships between children and
their working mothers can be better and more

relaxed than those experienced by 'non-working'
mothers whose non-stop contact with their
children can be boring or fraught. Of course all
children complain at times about the way they're
treated. It's an excellent ploy for arousing guilt in
a working mother if her children moan about her
absence and compare their lot with that of friends
whose mothers are always *there*. The full-time
mother's children may equally complain about
their mother's over-involvement, saying they wish
their mother would go out to work and leave
them alone! Experienced parents know that at
times they can't win.

Once the children are past needing constant
care, the fact that they have to look after
themselves to a large extent can enable them to
grow up self-reliant and sensible. Their parents
are always available when they're needed but
there's little question of smother-love.

If you feel warm towards your children, and
they towards you, there's no need to accept the
load of guilt that other people are so ready to pile
onto the working mother (especially if she's got
an interesting job!). In the 1990s more and more
middle-aged women are going to be needed in the
workforce. Many will have teenage or young adult
children. There's no evidence that these children
will be more likely to be delinquent or disturbed
than those of stay-at-home mothers. But we must
be prepared for the usual backlash that occurs
whenever women claim their right to equal
opportunities.

Q  **It's extraordinary how we have such poor
relations with one of our children and get on
so well with the other. We think we've always
treated them the same.**

A  Most parents bend over backwards to treat their
children equally. The trouble is, of course, that all
children are different – in age, possibly in sex,

physical constitution, ability, personality – and
these differences have little to do with the way
we've treated them. Even in babyhood we can
notice differences: one three-week-old infant
sleeps sweetly all night. Her sister, two years later,
screams inconsolably for hours. The parents who
have been congratulating themselves on how well
they've managed their first daughter, have their
confidence rudely shattered by the non-
co-operation of the second. It's the same through
childhood and beyond.

Clearly a wise parent won't lavish attention and
toys on one child and neglect the other. But in all
sorts of subtle ways she may be showing extra
care and extra attention to one child, and the
other is quick to perceive this. The excuse may be
that the 'favoured' one is younger, more delicate,
has a more fragile personality, or whatever. The
fact is that that child seems to be getting
something the other, possibly more apparently
robust one, isn't.

So tension and rivalry may build up and result
in rows and perhaps even rejection of the less-
favoured child which, of course, only makes
matters worse. This is one quite common reason
for a parent finding difficulty in relating to one
child, but no such problem with the other.

However, we do have to face the fact that it's
possible for there to be innate personality
differences that can influence the child's
behaviour towards her parents, and consequently
theirs towards her. We may feel a great sense of
responsibility towards all our children, and do
what we believe is best for them, but it's
impossible to love and *like* them all equally, or
even to share their interests. If we're interested in
the arts or the countryside and our child is mad
on computer games or skating, we'll probably be
glad to give her opportunities to follow her
hobbies, but it may prove impractical to share
them with her in a meaningful way. What we
have to avoid, in a case like this, is to give her the

impression that her interests are less worthy than
our own – they're just different.

Your daughters will probably turn out very
differently. There's nothing wrong with that: each
can be equally successful and effective in her own
way. And if each is encouraged to develop as a
separate, different person, relations between
parents and each child will have a chance to
develop in a relaxed and friendly atmosphere,
whether or not this is a particularly close one in
the future.

**Q** **My daughter is married to someone with
whom I just don't get on. I've done my best
to keep friendly with him, but he seems to
reject the relationship.**

**A** It's tough to feel that in some ways you seem to
be filling the mother-in-law joke role in his eyes.
Obviously you find it puzzling that he's taken
against you, because you can't see that there's
anything you have done to make him react like
this.

But there could be all sorts of reasons behind
his apparent hostility. First of all, it may be that
he is sensitive about your relationship with your
daughter. He may be jealous and possessive,
believing that if you get on well with her, she is
too dependent on you and that excludes
something that *he* should be getting from her. It
might be worth considering whether or not she
actually does depend on you too much, and if you
think she does, work on ways in which she can be
gradually weaned away from this dependency.
Naturally you won't want to break a close
relationship with your daughter, but a close
relationship needn't involve over-dependence. Your
son-in-law may be very insecure and for this
reason believes that his wife is threatening his
relationship with her by sharing her love with
anyone outside the marriage. Time may teach

him that his wife can love different people in different ways, and that you are no threat to him. But meanwhile you may have to tread extra carefully to avoid apparent interference in their lives, however well meant.

Of course there could be some forgotten incident that he has misunderstood or misinterpreted which has given him the wrong impression of you. Reflection may lead you to pinpoint this, and there may then be some way in which you can raise the matter with him and discuss the misunderstanding. That could clear the air.

Among other reasons for his suspicion of you there could be some class, religious or racial sensitivity. A man from a poor background may feel unnecessarily anxious if his wife comes from a more privileged family and vice versa. It's difficult for all of us to accept people as they are, regardless of educational or religious differences, but of course many marriages are enriched by acceptance into an extended family or different cultural groups.

Sometimes intolerance between the generations melts away once there are grandchildren. Children benefit so much from a close and loving relationship with their grandparents that many fathers forget their differences with their in-laws in order to foster that new and rewarding development.

Patience, a willingness to stand back a little, and acceptance of your son-in-law as a person are the only options you now have; meanwhile, this nagging worry will be largely dissipated if you get on with your own life. Cultivating one's interests, keeping up with friends, becoming a more independent person, are the best ways of countering family problems so that they become less emotionally draining.

Q **I enjoy looking after my grandchildren occasionally, but I'm beginning to feel my age. Two under-fives are so energetic. My daughter leaves them with me most days. She couldn't go to work without my back-up, so it's difficult to say 'no'.**

A Far too many grandmothers are having to step in to act as unpaid childminders because childcare provision is so lamentably lacking, especially in the UK, which has the worst childcare provision record in Europe. Local authority nursery provision covers only a tiny minority of working mothers. In middle-class areas privately-run nurseries and nursery schools do exist, but their fees are too high for most poorly-paid mothers. Their only remedy is the registered childminder, often a very caring, responsible person, but someone who herself is underpaid for what she does, simply because the working mother can't afford to reward her more adequately. Grandmothers often plug the gap, and because of their relationship feel they can't ask for more than out-of-pocket expenses or, as in your case, can't put the children's mother's employment at risk by trying to shift the burden elsewhere.

It is indeed hard that your daughter might have to give up work or curtail her hours if you decide that you can't carry on as you are. But really that's her problem, and it will only be solved if she is willing to try some other method of child-minding and, if she fails, get together with other working mothers to demand more local authority or workplace nurseries. Recent British Government pronouncements have made it clear that childcare in the future is to be in the hands of private enterprise. It has been suggested that industrial and commercial companies in a given area should get together to meet the needs of the mothers who are now going to be lured back into offices and factories to compensate for the lack of teenage recruits to industry in the 1990s.

Of course you feel involved in the welfare of your daughter and her children, but while no doubt you'd be glad to help out in an emergency, they're really not your responsibility. That was discharged when you made so many adjustments to your life in bringing up your own family. Looking after pre-school children is very tiring. You'd probably find a job outside the home much less demanding and, released from the present set-up, you might find it more permanently rewarding too.

**Q** **My son and his wife live just round the corner. He's not a very helpful husband, I'm afraid, so my husband, who is retired, is always being called in to do odd jobs, sometimes at very inconvenient times. This makes him irritable and he takes it out on me for having let the boy get away with it for all these years.**

**A** It may well be that you never asked your son to do a hand's turn in the home and that this has made him unwilling to take his share of domestic jobs. That was a mistake. But what was his father doing all that time? Children learn by example as well as precept, and if a father is never seen to be sharing the boring as well as the more rewarding jobs, it's hardly surprising that when they have homes of their own, young men will continue to expect to opt out. So if there's any blame, it has to be shared between you and your husband.

You can't relive the past, but your husband could now do two things. First, he could just refuse to help out if he has other plans for his time, telling his son that he'll come along when it suits him. But more constructive would be to actually show his son how to manage domestic crises and the inevitable odd jobs. He could help him to organize a selection of necessary tools, show him how to decorate a room, look after his car, do the gardening or other jobs for which help is so constantly sought. He could give him DIY books and magazines and suggest where he could get advice that wouldn't involve his father.

**Q** **I'm a widow, living alone. One of my daughters lives nearby and she visits me about twice a week. I know she'd like to do more for me than that, but I'm an independent sort of person and I don't need her help. How can I persuade her that I really can manage on my own?**

**A** It's good that your daughter wants to help you. It's good that you are independent and don't actually need anything more from your daughter than this regular contact. However, there are two points to be borne in mind. One is that by being too forceful about refusing help you may give her the feeling that you're rejecting her love and concern. The other is that the time may come when you really do need her; if you become ill or infirm it may be necessary for her to take over some responsibility for you, and if you've been too adamant about refusing help she may be hesitant about giving it or actually not perceive a need that you're too independent to ask her to meet.

If you can make very clear to her how greatly you appreciate her visits and how important contact with her is to you (sometimes we forget to tell people how much we care for them) that should dispel any feeling of rejection she may have. At the same time you could say that you know that there may come a time when practical help is needed, and promise that when that happens, you'll ask for it. That will relieve her mind and enable her to relax about you now.

Q I suppose our problem is one that some
people wouldn't see as one. It's simply that
bad blood has arisen between our two
daughters because each wants us to retire to
their town and they're hundreds of miles
apart. There's a lot to be said for either place,
but whichever one we choose, the other
daughter is going to be jealous.

 You're right – some people would be flattered to
be fought over like this! Your daughters must be
very fond of you to want to have you living
nearby, and it may be, too, that each can see
advantages to herself in having the older
generation close at hand.

Depending on your state of health and strength,
one possible solution could be to decide to live
half-way, or thereabouts, between the two towns.
That would make each family relatively
accessible and not commit you too heavily to
either.

Perhaps another solution would be to draw up a
balance sheet. Are house prices and living
expenses similar in each area, or are they so
different that one would cripple you financially
while the other would be more manageable? Is
one place better served by public transport (vital if
you may not have a car in the future)? What
about the health service and local hospitals?
What about proximity to old friends? These are
the sorts of questions that should be asked by
anyone thinking of retiring to a new area, and the
answers could be crucial.

In your case there are other, family
considerations, too. Does either of your daughters
have particular family difficulties that would
override the needs of the other to have her parents
living nearby? Perhaps one of them is working
outside the home while the other is not: the
former would find grandparents very useful in
school holidays or as occasional sitters. And what

about your sons-in-law? Do you get on with one better than you do with the other?

What this situation seems to call for is a family conference. You could draw up your balance sheet first, and this might provide absolute proof that the advantages of moving to town A are so great that they rule out town B; you'd then just have to convince your daughters of the validity of this conclusion. At the same time you would have to reassure the 'unsuccessful' daughter that your decision was taken on these rational grounds, that it was regrettable that you couldn't be in two places at once, but that you'd make every effort to visit and be visited in the future. And that's where your other daughter could be drawn in: to accommodate visitors, you'd probably have to split the visiting family between two dwellings, so co-operation would be needed. But it would enable the sisters to see more of each other and, most important, enable their children to make regular contact with their cousins.

Probably there's more than a touch of 'sibling rivalry' behind your daughters' quarrels on this issue: it may have a long history. Maybe it's never been possible to solve their disagreements and rivalries in a rational way. Here would be a chance to heal the rift by an appeal to reason, so enabling them to put childish jealousies behind them and grow up.

## Q I'd like to be a good grandparent, but I don't feel like a granny at all. After all I'm only 42.

A Since many women are now having babies in their late thirties and early forties, you probably know women of your age whose babies are your grandchild's contemporaries. Nowadays many grandmothers, whether they're in their forties or their sixties, don't behave like the traditional granny. They're too busy earning a living and leading their own lives to be sitting by the fire knitting tiny garments.

Very probably you won't be able to give as much time to your daughter and her family as the 'traditional' granny did. There are some disadvantages, of course (you won't be such a useful baby-sitter if you're too busy or live too far away), but there are considerable advantages, too. Your daughter isn't likely to be smothered by over-concern for her baby and herself, lavished on her by an underoccupied grandmother. And, as her children grow up, visits and outings to a relatively young, energetic and interesting grandmother will be a lot of fun.

A good grandmother isn't easy to define; as in all relationships, it's an individual thing. There are only a few guidelines. A flexible attitude is probably the most important. If your daughter's ways of bringing up her children are different from yours, that's her business. Advice can be given, of course, but only if it's asked for. There's really no right or wrong way in baby and childcare. Fashions change, and most mothers are anxious to do the right thing in the light of contemporary theory and practice. Maybe it is just fashion; or maybe knowledge has in fact advanced since you had your children. You can only go along with your daughter's ideas, and try to behave consistently with them when you are with the child.

Grandmothers are often treasured confidants of older children, and that warm and trusting relationship is something to be cultivated right from the beginning. Whatever your reservations about the way the children are cared for, they should see you as supportive and relaxed friends of their parents, with background and experiences in common, to complement the diversity inevitable between the generations.

**Q** **My grandchildren live far away. We can't afford to visit very often, and their parents are too busy, in any case, to take time off. It's difficult to maintain the relationship.**

**A** Telephone calls, though costly, are a lot cheaper than travel. A weekend call, initiated by each family in turn, can share the cost; or perhaps your son is better off and could pay the bills. You could make sure to have a few words with each child to find out what he or she is doing and express your affection. A weekly postcard to each child in turn is often appreciated. Some children keep attractive cards in an album or on a pinboard in the bedroom as a constant reminder of their grandparents. Once they're old enough, of course, they'll be able to visit you on their own. If the journey involves no train changes and the children have done it with parents in the past, they should be able to manage it by themselves, providing their parents put them into a carriage already occupied by plenty of responsible-looking adults, and you make sure to meet them at the other end. If the journey is at all complicated, of course, they may have to wait until they're a bit older before travelling alone.

Naturally it's more difficult to keep contact with family at a distance, and they won't be as closely involved with you as they would be if they lived in the next street. But in some families, distance lends enchantment, and family visits are all the more treasured because they're necessarily less frequent.

Q   **Our son and his wife divorced recently, and she has their two children living with her and her new husband. We were devoted to the children, who saw a lot of us. But since her remarriage she won't allow them to make contact. What can we do?**

A   If your son can't intervene, unfortunately you have little option but to continue to press your former daughter-in-law to let you see your grandchildren and hope that she will relent. Possibly she has the idea that a clean break with your family is in the children's best interests, but actually research has shown that maintaining contact with an extended family is emotionally beneficial to the children of divorced parents, who appreciate the continuity with grandparents, especially if the relationship has been a good one.

Sadly this is not an uncommon situation, and there's an organization in the UK specially concerned with the problems of grandparents who want to re-establish contact with their grandchildren. It's called the National Association of Grandparents;* in the US a similar group is called Grandparents'-Children's Rights, Inc.* These bodies can offer advice and information about your legal rights – if any.

Q   **I'm in the strange position of having stepchildren a little older and a little younger than myself. It seems silly, but they don't appear to know what to call me. 'Mother' or 'Mum' both seem ridiculous in the circumstances.**

A   Since very many adults and teenagers now call their natural parents by their first names, this simple solution could be adopted in your family. You could just tell them you expect to be called by your first name in the future, and unless they

want to maintain a distant relationship for some
reason, that's the name they'll willingly adopt.

**Q** **I've done my best to make friends with my
teenage stepchildren, but they remain distant
or even hostile. I do want to get closer to
them. How can I break the ice?**

**A** Step-parenting is often very difficult indeed and
much depends on the circumstances behind the
situation. If their parents were divorced, the
teenagers will probably still be keeping contact
with their natural mother, and this may be
influencing their attitudes. If your husband was
widowed, the children may still be mourning the
death of their mother, and could see you as an
unwelcome interloper in the family. The great
variety of circumstances means that there's no
one cause and no one solution to the problem.

It's useful to remember, too, that teenagers can
be difficult whatever the family circumstances.
Many happily married couples who provide a
good and stable home for their natural children do
nevertheless go through all sorts of adolescent
traumas, and actual hostility towards parents is
just one manifestation of the difficulties in
adjustment to growing up that so many young
people experience.

The only advice that can be given, and it
applies to your husband as well as to yourself, is
'go slow'. Don't expect instant acceptance and
love; do expect mutual respect and a degree of
tolerance. Ground rules have to be established,
and they obviously include a banning of name-
calling, threats, and actual violence.

In most countries there are now national
organizations for step-parents and their children.
The National Stepfamily Association* in the UK
and the Stepfamily Association of America* are
self-help groups with publications and local
counsellors. Organizations for single parents can
also refer you to local groups.

# Further reading

*And You Thought It Was Over: Mothers and Their Adult Children* Zenith Henkin Gross (New York: St Martin's Press)

*The Good Step-parents Guide* Ruth Inglis (Grafton Books)

*Help! I've Got a Teenager* Robert T. Bayard and Jean Bayard (Exley)

*Ourselves and Our Children* Boston Women's Health Book Collective (Penguin)

*Parenthood: The Whole Story* Dorothy Einon (Bloomsbury)

# 6   Coping with crisis

**Q** **My partner died three months ago. At first I
felt numbed. Then I had various legal matters
to clear up. Now I feel devastated. Shall I ever
recover?**

**A** It's recognized nowadays that bereaved people
usually go through several stages of grief and
mourning. You experienced the first stage when
everything seemed unreal and you couldn't feel
anything – or wouldn't allow yourself to. That got
you through the first few days. After that you had
so much to do that you lived from hour to hour,
pushing the pain away. That stage is behind you
and the full force of your loss has hit you.

Of course you feel devastated and bereft. People
who have made a study of bereavement say that
it's very important at this time to accept how you
feel, acknowledge what your partner meant to
you, talk about him with friends and relatives,
remember the good things you did together and
realize that there were also some bad patches,
some actions you now wish could be undone.
Some people may seem to shy away from you
once the funeral is over, and indeed many people
find it terribly difficult to cope with someone
else's grief. But there are others who are only too
anxious to do something to help you, but don't
know how. Don't feel you're imposing too much
on them if you ask for support. Sensitive friends
will know that you really do need to be allowed

to cry and they'll help you to express what you feel. Three months after a loss like yours it's inevitable that you will often have days and nights when the grief seems intolerable and never-ending. Acceptance that this is an almost universal reaction, not weakness, may help you. If you have no close friends with whom to talk about your loss and share your grief in some measure, there are organizations that can help by putting you in touch with counsellors and groups of people who have gone through your experience and will understand how you feel. Cruse* and the National Association of Widows* in the UK and the National Association for Widowed People in the US offer help in facing grief and loneliness, and can also offer advice on individual and practical problems. Elsewhere, contact women's organizations for advice about counselling agencies.

With support from others you will gradually recover from this present despair, but it's a process that can't be hurried. It's often said that it takes two years to recover your balance, but of course it very much depends on the individual personality, how much the dead person meant to the bereaved one, and the circumstances in which she finds herself. The main point is that she needs time – time to accept the loss, to express anger and frustration about what has happened, to express regret at what she may see as opportunities lost while the person was alive. So the 'two years' is simply an average period for recovery; it could be more, or less.

You can't expect everything to return to normal, if by normal you mean the way you lived before your partner died. Obviously that's impossible. What you can expect is a gradual picking up of the threads and a rebuilding of your life in changed circumstances. Life will be different: there could even be some positive elements in it. However difficult it is for you now to believe that you will come through, that will happen. It can't be hurried. Suppression of feelings can only slow the process, so don't try.

**Q** **Since my husband died I've had a lot of help from my sons and daughters and from neighbours, too. But now I realize I can't go on relying on other people to give practical help. The trouble is that I've never been involved in money matters or DIY and I feel quite useless.**

**A** It's a sad fact that far too many women accept that they're no good at managing money or doing household repairs, and all too many men accept that these matters are *their* affairs. This may mean division of labour with each partner having a particular function in the running of the home, but it also means that if a man loses his wife he hasn't the faintest idea how to cook, wash, iron and keep the house clean. And if the woman is widowed, she finds herself in your position.

The best thing you can do now would be to continue to accept the help you've been getting, but only in a learning capacity. You could ask your neighbour to show you how to unblock a drain rather than leave him to do it for you. You could ask your daughter to sit down with you and run through the mechanics of organizing your accounts, dealing with the bank and the building society and your taxes. You can ask for advice about suitable books and leaflets to help you with a variety of practical problems, and then try out their suggestions yourself.

If you have good relations with your legal adviser, bank manager or accountant, they will often prove very helpful, and the charges, if any, will be offset by your increasing ability to cope on your own.

The bonus in all this will be increasing self-confidence and a pride in your ability to lead an independent life. It's never too late to move from over-dependence towards self-sufficiency, and the material and emotional rewards that it brings.

Q **My story is almost a cliché. My husband left me for my so-called best friend. Now my hatred for her is so intense it seems to be destroying me.**

A You're trying to cope with a double betrayal. Your husband's abandonment of you was hard enough to deal with, but things are made immeasurably worse by the fact that your friend was involved. You probably believe that you can never trust anyone again.

This will be a difficult situation to sort out. Perhaps you are concentrating your hatred upon your former friend because it's easier to blame her than your husband for what has happened. If you accept that he has equal responsibility with her for the break-up of your marriage perhaps you would have to accept that there was something missing in the marriage to start with – something you'd prefer not to face. Making her a scapegoat enables you to avoid that issue.

It's too much to expect that in the light of a reappraisal of your husband and of your relationship with him you'll immediately be able to accept that if there's any blame, it has to be shared between them and, possibly, yourself. It's unlikely that your husband is so weak that he could be lured away by this siren; some series of events, difficulties, misunderstandings could lie behind his decision to leave you, and hers to leave *her* husband. Her motives could be very mixed: perhaps her own marriage was on the verge of collapse, and she desperately needed the security a new man might represent; perhaps she needed to persuade a man to leave his wife for her. You won't be able to forgive her, probably, for what she has done, but you may be able to understand what lay behind her decision. And that understanding could take a lot of the heat out of your consuming hatred for her.

Hatred *is* destructive. It can distort not only the way we see other people but also make us do things that we afterwards regret. It's easy to say that we ought to ride above it and love our enemies, but very, very hard to practise. Yet if we realize that this hatred is actually doing us far more harm than we're doing to the object of it, we can try to think and behave rationally. You may have to accept what has happened, because nothing you can now do will change the situation. In those circumstances, your intense feelings of hatred can only make everything worse for you, delaying both the coming to terms with your loss and sense of betrayal, and the beginning of a look to a future. For of course there is a future, and the end of your marriage doesn't mean the end of you.

**Q** **We were very young when we married. We got on reasonably well for years, then suddenly decided that the excitement and fun had gone out of the relationship. We divorced, but looking back on it, our reasons seem pretty trivial. How could I have let it happen?**

**A** You both let it happen. No one would want to return to the past when convention kept unhappy couples together for a lifetime of misery, but you now seem to believe that a little more effort, and a little more reflection about what the relationship was really about, could have saved the marriage.

But you made a mistake – if mistake it was – and now you're having to accept it. When no children are involved, the break-up of a marriage usually has few serious consequences except for the couple themselves. You now regret what happened but, older and wiser, you can go on to build a new life, perhaps find a new relationship. Looking back won't help, except insofar as it will enable you to avoid making far-reaching decisions without a lot of thought and reflection.

Your experience may be very useful, too, for friends who might be in the same situation as you were. As a divorced person you're very likely to be involved in discussions about other people's marriages; perhaps you'll be asked for direct advice. Although you'd never want to tell your friends what to do, it may be that you'll feel able to suggest that they think very carefully when they consider divorce. There's little doubt that when there are young children involved, their need for both parents would override any vague feelings of irritation or dissatisfaction between husband and wife, and such a realization may pull the marriage back from the brink.

**Q** **Whenever we go to a party or out with another couple, my husband pays much more attention to someone else's wife than he does to his own! Am I silly to mind?**

**A** Justifiably or not, you *do* mind. Even if you believe that his flirtatious behaviour is superficial, you can still feel humiliated, and your husband should be able to see this. If he won't appreciate how you feel, and change his behaviour in consequence, perhaps you can find a way of drawing attention publicly to what is happening. But of course this would have to be done in a lighthearted and humorous way, putting the onus on him rather than the object of his flirtations.

Some men, and women, who are rather insecure about themselves do try to boost their egos and reassure themselves that they are still attractive by acting in this provocative way. Usually such self-inflation has only harmless consequences, but if a partner finds it upsetting, that's a good enough reason to behave in a more mature fashion.

**Q** Unbelievably, I'm still allotted the same housekeeping money as I had three years ago, despite inflation and the fact that the children are older. When I complain, I'm told I'm a bad manager.

**A** Generalized complaints seem to have failed. Now it looks as though you need to produce chapter and verse to show how difficult, or impossible, it is to manage on an allowance that may have been adequate three years ago, but isn't now.

Your partner's head must have been in the sand if he isn't aware of price rises, and if he acts as though as children grow their needs remain static. It may convince him if you can keep detailed accounts for a week or two to show him how much everything costs; or better still, take him shopping for food and the children's clothes. If he still believes that you ought to be able to manage on the current 'housekeeping' you could challenge him to take over the shopping and see whether he can do better. Unless you are, in fact, a poor manager, he'll either spend much more than you do on the grocery and other bills, or find that by the end of the week the fridge is empty following his attempt to keep within the present limits.

All this, of course, assumes that the family income has at least kept pace with current prices. If a change of job or unemployment has resulted in a reduced income, naturally the picture is different. It will then be a question of sitting down together and working out just how the money is to be allotted. Priorities, after fixed outgoings such as rent or mortgage, and fuel bills, would be food and clothing with other expenses adjusted to match current income. And that means adjusting *everyone's* expenses; if so-called luxuries have to be cut out, this applies to all the family.

As with so many family disagreements, it should be possible to solve this problem by talking unemotionally about it, basing your arguments on facts, not general complaints and accusations. Easier said than done if you've been battling with this difficulty without success, but it really is the only way.

Q **We're quite comfortably off, but I need a job. It isn't the money, it's the interest and companionship I want. But my husband is totally opposed.**

A Like many men, he's probably got all the arguments ready. The most familiar is that the family will suffer if a mother goes out to work. Then there's the suggestion that there's something wrong with a woman who doesn't find total satisfaction in her mother-housewife role. Finally (though this argument is wearing a lot thinner nowadays) there's the 'a man's pride is affected if he can't keep a wife and family' line.

Take the first, and apparently most powerful, argument. Is it the family (that is, the children) who will suffer? Or is it the so-called head of the household who might find himself having to adapt to doing a lot more for himself if his wife isn't there to do it for him? What's more, he'd have no excuse not to take a much more active part in caring for the children. No longer could it be seen as the mother's job alone, if she, like himself, has responsibilities outside the home.

All the evidence is that if children are well cared for during their parents' working hours, and the parents take fair shares in running the home, the family actually benefits. Of course there are problems to be faced – good childcare facilities aren't easy to find – but these problems can be shared: it shouldn't be the mother who takes all the responsibility for the children, the meals and the housework.

Some women do find fulfilment in raising a family and running a home. But women whose horizons are wider aren't abnormal, just different.

And such women are becoming more visible, more vocal. Many enjoy the mental stimulation of a challenging job, or enjoy working alongside others as part of a team. They appreciate the independence and the feeling of achievement and self-respect that work engenders. And if this means, as it so often does, that they're happier people, the family too will benefit.

The masculine pride argument won't wash at a time when such a high percentage of women now work outside the home. Far from being able to claim satisfaction at being able to keep a wife and family, a man who won't allow his wife to go out to work will be seen as a strange hangover from the past.

**Q** **It's difficult to persuade my husband that it isn't a slight on him that I enjoy my evening class and the occasional outing with friends. He has no interests outside work and family – I have.**

**A** Many couples whose interests and friends are different can manage to reach a sensible compromise. A separate once-a-week evening out for each is balanced by another evening when they do something together. Assuming that no baby-sitting is needed, if the partners each do their own thing on the same night of the week, they'll see that much more of each other on the other evenings.

Your situation may be different, but really there seems to be no reason why you have to adapt to the lifestyle preferred by your husband. It's not at all unreasonable for you to want to pursue your interest at an evening class and to keep up with old friends. You aren't inconveniencing him in any way by this very moderate amount of solo activity; apparently you're not forcing incompatible people upon him either. If he prefers to stay at home, and you prefer to do something

else, you both have the right to follow your
individual preferences. No doubt you'd be pleased
if he, too, took up some absorbing hobby or
outside interest – but that would be up to him.

If you were gadding out every night, without
thought for his feelings or comfort, he might have
a case for believing that you no longer cared about
him. As things are, it seems right that you should
assert your needs, which are presumably just as
strong as (though different from) his own.

**Q** **He's a keen angler. I used to accompany him
on his weekend fishing trips, but now we
have the children I can't. It was boring
anyway! But it seems unfair that I'm stuck at
home and we hardly see him at weekends.**

A In a relationship where the children are seen as
the mother's responsibility, it's all too often the
case that she is the one who has to adapt to being
a parent, while the father just carries on as before.
This inability to face up to the reality of
parenthood must be a major cause of marriage
breakdown.

If pointing out the obvious fails, as sadly it
often does in such a case, the only solution would
seem to be to attempt to cultivate your own
interests, limited as you may be by having to
accommodate the children's needs. Other angling
widows and their children might get together, for
instance, for picnics and excursions. Inevitably
you will have to accept the distancing that these
weekend separations entail.

Women who feel they've suffered this kind of
neglect may be able to do little about their own
situation, but they can do something to change
the behaviour of future generations. They can
encourage daughters to act much more
independently than they did themselves. If you
didn't enjoy spending your weekends parked
beside an angler you presumably did so because

that sort of submissive behaviour was expected of you. Your daughter needn't follow this example. A boy should be able to learn that he isn't automatically the boss in any relationship – there has to be give and take. He must also learn that parenthood is a joint responsibility; if he prefers fishing or playing sport to being a father, he shouldn't have children.

**Q** **I've always been 'just a housewife'. In fact I've done everything in the house while my husband was at work. Now he's retired, but he still leaves everything to me. I'd like to put my feet up sometimes, too.**

**A** If ever there was a time when such division of labour was justified, it isn't now. Assuming that your husband's health is reasonably good, he should be able to do more than *help*. You should be able to divide the housework, shopping and cooking between you. It may be that as a result of your years of experience you're a far better cook than he ever would be, but that shouldn't prevent him learning to prepare a simple meal. He could also learn to share the weekly shopping; he could buy the fruit and vegetables (with a list, at first) while you get the groceries, for instance. But it would be wise for him to come with you a few times while you do your part of the shopping, so that he gets an idea of requirements and prices. He could also learn to use the vacuum cleaner, the washing machine and other household appliances. This would mean that not only would he be able to do a fair share of the work, but also he'd be able to take over for a while if you were ill – an increasing possibility as we get older. At the same time, it would be as well for you to familiarize yourself with any job that he has normally done, like keeping accounts or cleaning the car.

Once he's acquired some of these new skills,

you'll probably find that work-sharing becomes a routine. He could make the lunch and you cook the supper; he'd vacuum the carpets while you dust and polish, and so on.

The bonus from sharing the responsibilities will be that not only will you each be better prepared to do the other's job in an emergency, but you'll have much more time to enjoy your leisure together, not just put your feet up, but get out and about and do the sort of things neither of you had time for before.

**Q** **My mother lives with us and has recently become totally disabled. I had to give up my job to look after her. I'm drawing all the social security to which we're entitled, but I get desperate at times with the 24-hours-a-day responsibility. What practical help could I expect, and where?**

 Your problem is becoming increasingly common, with an ageing population and current policies which encourage so-called care in the community. The *community*, as you've found, is you.

If you aren't in touch with the voluntary organization concerned with your mother's particular disability, do contact it. The Alzheimer's Disease Society* in the UK and the Alzheimer's Disease and Related Disorders Assocation* in the US; the Royal National Institute for the Blind* and the American Foundation for the Blind* are among the many such organizations. These bodies give information and support, and can often put you in touch with local groups or suggest other sources of help.

There are also organizations specifically set up for carers such as yourself. Many women in your position find contact with others invaluable, not only because they provide an outlet for social contact and expression of frustrations, but because members can offer each other mutual support over a range of practical matters. They

also campaign for a better deal for carers. The
Association of Carers* is the British organization;
in the US contact the Children of Ageing Parents*
and the National Council on the Ageing* which
has a Family Caregivers Program.

One of the most important functions of some
organizations is the provision of respite care.
Some local authority residential or nursing homes
in the UK may be able to accommodate your
mother for a while to enable you to take a
holiday, but places are very limited and waiting
lists invariably long. A charitable agency such as
Counsel and Care for the Elderly* and Elderly
Accommodation Counsel* can advise on private
nursing homes, some of which are prepared to
take old people for a short stay, but of course fees
are high. The Marie Curie Memorial Foundation*
has some short stay places in their nursing homes
for cancer sufferers.

In many areas the local social services can
arrange for elderly people who have some
mobility to attend a day care centre. If your
mother were offered a place and could make use
of the transport which may be provided, she could
be cared for by experienced paid or voluntary
workers for a few hours each day, and would
benefit from the companionship of others. This
would give you the regular respite you obviously
need.

Q **I've exhausted all the possibilities of help
from organizations, social services, friends
and relatives; now it has become impossible
to look after my husband at home. I am
totally exhausted and I think I could be on
the verge of cracking up myself. But I still
feel terrible about the idea of getting him
admitted to a geriatric ward.**

A Most people do look upon the geriatric ward as a
last resort – as indeed it is. But there does come a

time when it is no longer possible for someone who is herself in her sixties or seventies to do all the practical jobs involved in looking after a helpless person. If she can't afford a considerable amount of paid help in the house, sadly and reluctantly she has to accept that she can no longer cope.

Your doctor or health visitor, who know you, your husband and your home conditions, will almost certainly agree that the only answer now is a hospital ward, and will be able to arrange for admission. Perhaps the fact that they perceive the need and know that there is really no alternative will enable you to come to terms with what has to happen. It may be of some comfort to you to realize that if your husband was capable of making the decision for himself, he would agree that this is the only solution. He would not want you to suffer a physical or mental breakdown in what are probably his last weeks of life. He would want you to remember him as he was in former years.

# Further reading

*Bereavement: Studies of Grief in Adult Life* Colin Murray Parkes (Penguin)

*Care for the Carer* Christine Orton (Thorsons)

*Confusion in Old Age* Dr J. P. Watts (BMA/Thorsons)

*Helping the Widowed* Margaret Torrie (Cruse)

*On Your Own: A Practical Guide to Independent Living* Jean Shapiro (Pandora)

*A Woman in Your Own Right* Anne Dickson (Pan)

# 7 Where to live

**Q** **Now I'm getting older, should I move or stay put?**

**A** There's a lot to be said for remaining in a neighbourhood you know, near to friends and, perhaps, your family. On the other hand, if your house is too large for you to manage easily, and if your health is giving you some cause for anxiety, it would seem sensible to sell up and find a house where housework, gardening and maintenance would be less demanding.

As with so many difficult decisions, it might be a good idea to sit down with a pencil and draw up a balance sheet. On the plus side there would be all the factors that might make life easier for you. On the minus side would be the expense of moving which should never be underestimated, because not only do you have to take into account the actual costs of transporting your furniture etc., legal fees and estate agent's commission, but all the hidden extras like new curtains, the cost of installing kitchen appliances, and the dozens of small items you inevitably have to replace. Some people find that any cash gained by selling a large house and buying a small flat is swallowed up by all the expenses involved. So if you are expecting to make money over the change, this could turn out to be a false hope.

Q **Everyone says I ought to move to a small flat, but I'd have to part with many of my possessions and I'm just not used to living in cramped surroundings.**

A Of course it's hard to part with furniture and other possessions that may have sentimental value. And if you've been used to a lot of living space, adapting to life in one or two rooms may prove difficult. But when age or infirmity make it sensible to consider something smaller, your health is surely more important than your belongings, and you might get a lot of pleasure out of refurnishing and re-equipping a new home, and exchanging large, old-fashioned pieces for modern, space-saving ones.

The one reason for not considering a really small place is if there's a likelihood of family or friends coming to stay. One spare room, however small, would then be well worth having. But failing that, you could replace an existing sofa with a sofa bed, and there are quite cheap camp beds that are surprisingly comfortable and which fold up for storage.

Q **Since my husband died I've had a problem keeping up with the gardening he used to do. I can't afford a gardener.**

A This quite common problem for older women can be solved by matching your need for help with someone else's need for a garden! You could advertise for someone – perhaps an active pensioner – to look after your garden in return for a share of the produce he or she grew in it. There are many keen gardeners whose circumstances are such that they have no garden at all, or a tiny one that doesn't give them enough to do.

You'd have to be prepared for the garden to be laid out to provide space for vegetables and fruit, but to offset these possible changes you'd get a supply of fresh produce, thus not only saving money but providing a healthy diet.

Q **My husband and I have recently had a splendid holiday in a favourite seaside town. We feel we need a complete change of scene when he retires next year, and house prices there seem manageable. Would we be wise to move?**

A If you're both well and active, you probably would enjoy a few years in this new attractive environment. But disasters can happen; and even if they don't, it could be that in your seventies and eighties you would need to be nearer to your family, and in need, too, of the health and social services that may be overstretched in an area where there are many older people. Somewhere that looks bright, clean and attractive on a balmy summer's day can take on a very different aspect in the cold and damp of winter, when amenities are closed down and the only people to be seen are the elderly and infirm.

Why not spend a few days in the town in the off-season, to get an idea of what it looks like then? Talk to local people to find out what services there are for older people, and what clubs, local associations and adult education facilities. And try to project the worst: how would it be in future years if one of you were widowed? What would your family feel, for instance, if they felt responsible for your welfare but were hundreds of miles away?

Many couples who moved in a spirit of great optimism to the seaside home of their dreams become quite disillusioned but can't afford to move back. This applies even more forcefully to those who have settled in sunnier climes – Spain or Portugal, for instance. Air fares prevent family and friends visiting very often; medical services may be rather different from those in the UK; and

isolation can be a real problem if fellow-
expatriates aren't compatible and there are
difficulties in integrating with the local
community.

Q **We really miss our grown-up children, both of
whom live hundreds of miles away. We're
fortunate because we both have freelance jobs
we could do anywhere so we could move to
be near to our son or daughter. They'd be glad
to have us. Should we go?**

A You're potentially mobile – but so are your
children. Young people do move around the
country quite a bit these days. You wouldn't want
to settle near to one of them, only to find that she
or he was offered a job somewhere else and was
thus placed in the position of letting you down or
refusing a good job, on your account.

You could be left high and dry in a strange
town, with no particular reason for being there. If
you're prepared to take that risk, and feel
adaptable enough to move yet again if necessary,
your next problem will be to decide which of
your children you want to be near – not an easy
decision! A compromise might be to fix on a spot
roughly half-way between the two, so that visits
would be easier than they are now.

Q **We don't want to move, but we're rattling
around in our large house which is becoming
increasingly costly to keep up. Should we
take a lodger?**

A Assuming that the family house has plenty of
spare rooms once your children have left home,
this is an idea worth considering. Of course
there's always the danger that the well-spoken,
apparently sensible, applicant for your room could
turn out to be a noisy, troublesome individual

whose rent was always in arrears, and that getting rid of her or him could pose all sorts of personal and legal difficulties. A necessary precaution is to take up references and insist on payment in advance, and to make sure that you understand what your own and your tenant's rights are. Your public library or Citizens Advice Bureau will provide you with leaflets.

Some people have found that a good solution is to take a student lodger from a local university, polytechnic or other college. He or she is with you only in term-time (you reserve the room in return for a reduced rent when they're on vacation) and, since you make arrangements through the college's accommodation office, if you meet trouble the office should intervene. At worst, the arrangement holds good only for the academic year.

**Q** **My friend and I are both divorced. We each own a flat. We've thought about selling up and buying something large that we could share. Will this work out?**

**A** It could be a solution to loneliness and encourage a sharing of responsibilities. If you feel that you know each other well enough – the possible foibles and snags as well as the friendship – the idea certainly is worth considering. But each of you has to be prepared for major adjustments, the sort of adjustments that we all have to make when sharing a home, whether with a sexual partner, parent or friend. Small differences can loom large, so you do have to have some basic agreement about meals, housework, payment of bills and so on, and it must be worked out ahead so that disagreement is kept to a minimum. Most women sharing a house or flat find that a bedsitter for each is a basic essential, even if there's also a shared living room, and that each should be able to entertain friends separately if these aren't mutual friends.

Given openness and a determination to make the arrangement work, it could be successful. But before committing yourselves financially you must be very sure that you don't have major reservations. Nothing is more miserable than breaking up a close friendship in these circumstances – unless it's breaking up a marriage.

Q **My father is on his own and rather unhappy. We both see too many possible snags in his moving in with me and my family. Would sheltered housing be the answer?**

A It might well be. Housing associations and private developers are providing increasing numbers of retirement homes in different parts of the country, some fairly large developments, others just a handful of houses and flats. Some schemes involve payment of an initial sum which the association or company pays back when the owner leaves or dies, without taking account of any intervening inflation. For example, if your father paid £50,000 for a flat and lived there for ten years, when he left he, or his heirs, would get only the original £50,000 for the property, although the market price (for which it could subsequently be sold) by then might be £100,000. There are other schemes with different financial arrangements. In all cases a service charge is payable, and it's important to get legal advice about liability, as some site owners put up service charges to unexpectedly high levels after a year or two.

The service charges usually include external maintenance of the building and gardens, the services of a warden who should be on call at any time to deal with emergencies, and sometimes the provision of communal lounges, etc. Some provide a restaurant and bar as well.

Your father could be much happier in a good development of this kind, where his neighbours would provide him with company and there would be someone to keep an eye on him. However, this sort of scheme is *not* suitable for someone who needs a lot of attention and nursing. Only a few private developments have residential or nursing homes on site for people who need more care as they get older than a warden can provide.

Once you've investigated the possibilities (make sure to read the Age Concern literature listed at the end of this chapter) you and your father should narrow down the list and visit each development to look at it with a critical eye. Then ask to be put on any waiting list and find out how long it's likely to be before the flat/bungalow will be available.

**Q** **The time has come for my mother to move into a residential home. You hear such horrific tales about them. How can we choose somewhere where she'll be comfortable and reasonably happy?**

**A** The media have indeed featured some places that are a disgrace to the local authorities or owners who run them. All 'homes' are supposed to be inspected by the local authority, which has the power to close down any where conditions don't meet a minimum standard. Unfortunately many local authorities' funds have been squeezed to the limit, and inspections aren't frequent, unless there have been complaints.

There is a code of practice to which all residential homes, whether run by private individuals, charities, or local authorities, are expected to adhere. However, you shouldn't assume that because the place is registered with the local authority you can choose it for your mother with confidence. You should read the Age

Concern information sheet listed below, visit several homes in your preferred area, preferably taking your mother with you, and ask questions.
Find out about:

activities and interests catered for;
involvement with the local community;
how much independence and freedom to come
   and go the resident is allowed;
number and quality of rules and regulations;
amount of privacy;
security for personal documents and
   possessions;
medical care – can your mother have her own
   GP?;
how much personal furniture etc. is allowed.

Once you've chosen a place, do make sure that your mother can have a trial period of about six weeks. She shouldn't give up her home until she's quite sure she's satisfied with the food, care and companionship offered in the residential setting.

Residential homes charge quite high fees, but if your mother's capital is less than £6,000 (1988 figure) she will qualify for residential care through the income support system. For details consult the fact sheet No. 11 from Age Concern.

**Q** **I am partially disabled, and my condition could get worse. I don't want to move into a home, though, as I value my independence. What help locally can I expect?**

**A** Your priority is to contact your local social services department. You should be visited by a social worker, who will assess your needs and, hopefully, arrange for them to be provided for, though this could take time. She or he may also suggest a visit from an occupational therapist, who can arrange for you to be given, or lent, suitable appliances to enable you to cook, bath, negotiate stairs and so on. The social worker may also arrange for you to have a home help, who will do basic housework and shopping as necessary.

If you are not already getting the social security allowances to which as a disabled person you may be entitled, ask the social worker to clarify the position for you, and to tell you what you should do to make sure of your full entitlements. It is in everyone's interests, as well as your own, that you stay put as long as you are able to manage at home, with help. Familiar surroundings, visits from friends and neighbours, and the feeling that despite some disabilities you're part of the community, can keep up your morale and contribute to your health and wellbeing in the future.

The social worker will be able to tell you about any day-care facilities in your area. Attending a centre each day would ensure that your medical and social needs were recognized and met. In some places transport is provided to enable people to attend the centres, but with shortage of funds this may not always be available.

Your doctor or social worker should also be able to arrange for meals-on-wheels to be delivered to your home if you are unable to cook or shop for one hot meal a day, and day care isn't suitable or available. It's up to everyone to find out about facilities and make full use of them.

## Further reading

*The Good Care Homes Guide* (Longman *with* Help The Aged)

*Home Life: A Code of Practice for Residential Care* (Centre for Policy on Ageing)

*The Legal Side of Buying a House* (Consumers Association)

*Your Housing in Retirement* (Age Concern)

The following Age Concern factsheets are free, in return for an s.a.e., from Age Concern:

*11 Income Support for Residential and Nursing Homes*

# 8 A positive future

**Q** **I need and want to work, but I've been at home for many years. What's available for a middle-aged woman?**

**A** The shortage of school-leavers is good news for you. For some time the Government has been making noises about the need for women 'returners' to fill the gap. So you could find that potential employers welcome you with open arms.

It may be that you need some form of brush-up training to bring your former skills up to date. Some companies are very glad to provide word-processing training for people who have been secretaries in the past and a few days *hands-on* experience is often quite enough to convert a typist into someone who's competent to use the new office technology. Someone who used to be a shop assistant isn't likely to need much training in the selling process but she, too, may need to learn to work on a new-style till and familiarize herself with new types of merchandise. This can be done on the job.

If your job was a professional one and you've been able to keep up with the publications in your field, you'll probably be ready to take on a new challenge. There's a perennial shortage of teachers with science qualifications, and if you're prepared to work rather hard at the beginning to keep several steps ahead of your students, you could soon be on top of your subject again. You may be a little rusty, but past experience and teaching skills won't have been lost. The same applies to many other jobs.

Often going out and looking for a job is a question of confidence. Don't underestimate the experience you've had in looking after a family and running a home. You've learnt a lot about human behaviour, personnel management, budgeting and account-keeping – all managerial skills. Many 'returners' are far more skilled at working with people than they were when they were younger. And employers nowadays often prefer a more mature person; for one thing, she's more likely to stay in a job, simply because it's much more difficult for her to move around the country than it is for a younger person with no domestic ties. You'll find, too, that employers are becoming more aware of the need to offer flexible hours to women with school-age children.

It's altogether a good time to be considering returning to work. Just let's make sure that when there's been another rise in the birth-rate and more teenagers on the job market, we don't get pushed back into the home again if we don't want to go. It has happened before.

**Q** **I stopped my training to get married. I really regret it now that I'm divorced and need to work. How can I get started again?**

**A** Depending on what kind of training it was, you could find that you can start where you left off. If your academic entry qualifications were sufficient before, you shouldn't need any further examination passes to enable you to re-enter training. One source of information would be your former college or training school (or its equivalent if you have moved). At the same time you could find out about any entitlement to a grant from the local education authority by contacting the local education office. In some circumstances 'mature' students do qualify for a grant, provided they didn't receive a full grant in their earlier years.

In some cases it may be more appropriate to find out about the availability of one of the government training schemes. It's difficult to be specific about these, because various schemes have come and gone, but a current one might suit you. Information in the first place is available from Job Centres.

Finally, do look at a good careers book which will tell you all you need to know about training for your particular career choice, the prospect for returners, part-timers, and a lot more basic information. *Equal Opportunities* (listed below) is a particularly comprehensive one.

**Q** **I'm in my fifties and completely untrained for any job. I don't really expect, or need, to get paid work, but I would like to learn something new and interesting. But is it worth it at my age?**

**A** The answer is that it's never too late. You're in a fortunate position because there is so much open to you, depending only on your personal interest, the local availability of educational and cultural courses, or how much time you're willing to give to *distance learning* (correspondence) courses.

It may be that you're really quite unsure how you would take to study, or even what sort of field you would like to enter. That's where a college of further education or polytechnic course aimed at people in your position could be so useful. Ask about New Opportunities for Women, Fresh Start or New Horizons courses (they go under different names in different places). Aimed primarily at people who're unsure about what they want to do and who may lack confidence in their ability to study, some of these courses are intensive, while

others are taken at a slower pace over a longer
period. Many women who've attended them have
found their interest aroused in subjects they'd
never considered before, and they've gone on to
study their chosen topic in greater depth at the
same college, a university, or local adult
education centre. Some who never intended to
train for a late-start career have been inspired by
one of these confidence-building courses to go on
to get the necessary qualification. It could happen
to you, too.

If study at a local college isn't feasible (you may
live in a part of the country where further
education institutions aren't accessible) there
should be an adult education centre nearer to
hand, and most of these offer a wide range of daytime or evening classes. If you really want to
widen your horizons, try something completely
different from the cooking, dressmaking and
similar domestic skills that such centres do offer.
You could opt for a foreign language, literature,
office training, keep-fit, painting, pottery,
sculpture, or music appreciation amongst others,
and meet some compatible fellow-students into
the bargain.

**Q** **Am I over-ambitious to be considering an
Open University degree?**

**A** Not if you're keen to learn, open-minded, and
willing and able to work quite hard over some
years in order to reach your goal. Open
University* students have to be dedicated enough
to set aside quite a lot of time each week for
individual study, be willing to get up early or go
to bed late to catch some of the OU programmes
on radio and TV, and be able to attend week-long
summer schools and regular study meetings
locally. However, they do receive a lot of help
from their tutors, reading material and study
notes which makes private study as painless as
possible.

You can be accepted for a degree course at any age and with few, or no, educational qualifications, though evidence that you're capable of sustained study is helpful. Every year women in their eighties are awarded OU degrees as well as younger women who have missed out on formal academic qualifications for all sorts of reasons.

If you're unsure about taking a degree course, the OU does offer a great range of shorter, less demanding courses – some vocational, some non-vocational. Take your pick from the publication describing these courses, which can last from a few weeks to about a year, and start at any time.

**Q** **I've heard about the University of the Third Age.\* What does this offer?**

**A** Primarily intended for retired people, the U3A movement, that started in France, has gained strength in the UK and in some other countries in recent years. A local branch of this organization is run by and for its members – there are no paid staff. No entrance qualifications are required, and there are no examinations.

Where membership is large enough, for example often in cities or university towns, it's run on the following lines: members volunteer to lead a group studying a chosen subject – philosophy, art, German, keep-fit, Shakespeare, history, economics or whatever – and may themselves attend another, completely unrelated study group led by another member, if they wish. Not everyone wishes, or feels qualified, to lead a group, but for an annual subscription (usually a modest one) an individual can attend as many groups as she or he likes.

Most U3As offer opportunities for social get-togethers, too, and study-visits to places connected with a particular course, at home or abroad, are a feature of many of the stronger ones.

London U3A, for instance, has a member who organizes cheap-rate holidays as far afield as China.

There are even groups for housebound members, with telephone links, so whatever your age and physical condition you could enjoy the opportunity of study with a lot of like-minded people. Most study groups are held during the day, thus avoiding evening or rush-hour travel. Wherever you live, there's likely to be a U3A somewhere near you. If there isn't, the head office can give you advice about starting one.

**Q** **I'm a full-time housewife and I don't think I'm a very good one. I'd like to improve my domestic skills.**

**A** Adult education centres, run by local education authorities, offer many courses in cooking, dressmaking and handicrafts. Perhaps you're being too modest. You probably know quite a bit about basic cooking, for instance, and what you may really need is new ideas and new styles of cooking – ethnic, vegetarian or budget, for instance. Most British adult education centres start their year in September, but in some places you can join at any time, provided there's a vacancy for you. Brochures and application forms are normally available either from your local centre or the public library about two months before the annual intake of students. Courses may be daytime or evening classes, and fees are moderate for people living in the local education authority's own area (they may be higher if you attend a class outside your own area).

Perhaps if you get into the habit of attending cookery or dressmaking classes you'll be inspired to try some of the other subjects on offer.

Q I don't think I can spare the time to get a regular job, but I'd like to do something. What opportunities are there for voluntary work?

A Since so many women nowadays are in full-time employment, in many places the reservoir of women available for voluntary work has run dry. So if you're able to offer help on a regular basis – even as little as a couple of hours a week – there will be a local organization that will welcome you.

Your public library should keep a list of local voluntary associations, and there may be a volunteer centre in the area which can give you a contact address and telephone number of an organization needing helpers. Or you could contact the headquarters of any organization known to you to get information about a local branch. The important thing is to choose an association with whose aims you are sympathetic, because you'll not only be happier working for a cause you support, but your fellow-volunteers will be compatible, too. The other proviso is that, except in case of illness or emergency, you must undertake to be completely reliable about whatever you agree to do. So don't promise too much at first. The organizers would much prefer you to do a little, regularly, than to promise to devote more time than you can really manage, and let everyone down by failing to turn up when expected. You can always extend your hours later on, when you're more familiar with the organization and feel more able to involve yourself in its work. And do offer to help with something that you're sure you're qualified to tackle – if you're hopeless at keeping accounts, for instance, don't be pushed into filling the vacant post of treasurer! You may be an excellent listener and counsellor, but no public speaker. Make that clear, so that everyone knows your strengths and limitations. But of course your abilities and confidence could develop, and then you'll be ready to seize later opportunities as they arise.

If you find the right niche you'll derive great satisfaction from filling some need in the community, which many women find a lot more rewarding than many kinds of paid work.

**Q** **Unexpectedly, I've been offered a wonderful job. But with children of 10 and 14, can I go to work full-time?**

**A** It would seem a pity not to accept this opportunity. How easily you can manage to cope with everything depends on a number of factors. First, what co-operation can you expect from your husband and the children? A working mother can't and shouldn't try to carry on with all her domestic jobs just as she did when she was at home every day. Your children are old enough to take some responsibility for cleaning and tidying their bedrooms, attending to their clothes, helping with shopping, laying and clearing the table and assisting with the washing-up. The older child should be able to prepare a simple meal. How well they do all this depends on how much responsibility they've been given in the past, but in any case, they should soon learn. Your husband, if he's convinced that for you resuming your former career is going to be emotionally satisfying as well as financially rewarding, will be willing to take a full share in the running of the house and caring for the children. He won't, hopefully, see it as *your* job to make sure everything runs smoothly.

Secondly, have you all the possible labour-saving equipment? If not, it would be worth earmarking the money you'll be earning to equip your home with items such as a microwave oven and a dishwasher. These things do save time and trouble.

Third, can you learn to tolerate easily-prepared

meals and convenience foods, leaving traditional
cooking to the weekends? Not all convenience
foods are of the 'cook-chill' variety which has
been given such a bad name recently. Frozen
dishes are both safe and tasty and the variety
available is increasing all the time.

Fourth, what about help in the home and/or
with the children? Paid help even for a half-day a
week can make a huge difference to the
cleanliness and tidiness of your home. And, since
you expect to be working normal office hours,
you'll probably need someone to keep an eye on
the children from the time they get home from
school until you or your husband return, to be
available if they're ill during term-time, and to be
there during school holidays unless you're able to
make arrangements with family or friends. Many
women have found that a 'motherly' older
woman, with experience of children and no
domestic ties herself, is willing to take on such a
flexible arrangement. Local advertising may well
result in applications from suitable people, and if
you find the right person the relationship can be
rewarding on both sides.

As you seem to have been 'head-hunted' you are
in a strong position to discuss with your employer
the need for you sometimes to take time off in
emergencies. And an understanding in advance
with your husband that it will be just as much
his responsibility as yours to take a child to the
doctor, attend a school sports day and supervise a
birthday party will ensure that it won't be a
question of *your* job, *his* career.

**Q** **I've been offered a job in my old workplace,
but I'm in my late forties and everyone there
is under thirty. Would I be out of place?**

**A** If you think of yourself as a stick-in-the-mud old
fogey, yes, you would be. But I doubt if you, or
anyone else, would describe herself in those

terms, whether she's in her forties or her seventies. The common experience of older people is that they never *feel* old.

Your skills may be a little rusty, but your past experience, and your greater knowledge of life, will more than make up for that. The young people you'll be working with will take you as they find you. Flexibility of attitude, an uncensorious approach to their ways of thinking and behaving, interest but not over-involvement in their preoccupations, dress that's reasonably fashionable but not extreme, and above all, competence at the job, will gain friendship and respect – not towards you as an older person, but as a fellow-worker who just happens to be older. Obviously you'll avoid seeming anxious to be 'one of the girls' when it comes to out-of-office socializing, but it probably won't be long before you're invited to lunch or an after-work drink with your colleagues, who'll take your presence as a matter of course.

Q  **I was made redundant when I was in my late fifties, and although I've applied for a number of jobs, no one wants to employ a woman who's nearly reached retirement age. I feel so useless.**

A  For many of us, our self-esteem is related to our ability to hold down a job. But many women, and men, are being told by employers and society in general that once they've reached, or almost reached, retirement age, they're no longer useful members of the community. It takes a lot of courage and hard thinking to resist these attitudes, but resist them we must.

Of course it's only being realistic to accept that in the eyes of a potential employer (though not in your own) you're too old to be given a job. That's a bitter pill to swallow, since you undoubtedly feel just as capable in every way as you were when you had a job. But it's counterproductive to allow yourself to become so obsessed with the unfairness of it all that you have no energy left for exploring the many possibilities that *are* open to you.

One woman who lost her job when the company she was working for was taken over by another organization spent several months getting more and more depressed about her position. She finally was forced to the conclusion that she wouldn't get another paid job in her specialized field, and looked about for ways in which her skill and experience could be utilized. The result was that she volunteered to work three mornings a week for an organization helping elderly pensioners; offered her skill and experience to a voluntary association which needed someone to keep the accounts but couldn't afford to pay a professional accountant; and attends a wood-carving class and a keep-fit group in what remains of her spare time. She's almost as busy as she was in her old job, and is actually enjoying the freedom of choice that she now realizes she's experiencing for the first time in her life.

**Q** **I've just retired – unwillingly – and I'm thinking of taking another job. Would I lose my UK retirement pension if I did?**

**A** At the time of writing, anyone who has reached retirement age but who wishes to continue to work for up to another five years can defer her or his pension; and it can be advantageous to do so, because the pension will have increased in the meantime. After the five years – that is at age 65 for a woman and 70 for a man – the pension is payable whether or not the person is working.

In 1989 the former *earnings rule* was abolished, so you will get your full pension even when you are in full-time employment and are receiving an income from that employment, unless you choose

to defer it. Therefore, it may well be worth your
while not to retire until you have to.

Social security regulations in Britain change
from time to time, but you can get current
leaflets from the public library, Citizens Advice
Bureau and Social Security office. Leaflet No. NI
32 *Your Retirement Pension,* and No. NI 92
*Earning Extra Pension by Cancelling Your
Retirement* are the ones you want.

Regulations about retirement in other parts of
the world are different: in some there's no
statutory retirement age, in others retirement age
depends on the individual's occupation.

Q **I'm an active woman in my forties. My
problem is finding a holiday where I won't
feel embarrassed to be on my own.**

A Certain tour operators offer some of their standard
package holidays for single travellers at special
times, (usually the less popular times of the year),
and this may mean that you get a double room for
the price of a single. Since your fellow-
holidaymakers are also singles, there won't be any
embarrassment. Of course there's no guarantee
that they'll all be compatible, but that's a risk you
may decide to take. Some people who have made
friends on holiday team up with them again – it's
largely a matter of luck.

If you enjoy sports or a walking holiday, you
could join a group organized by some of the
specialist firms such as the Holiday Fellowship.
Weekend and week-long courses in a variety of
subjects are listed in the publications of the
National Institute of Adult Continuing
Education.* Many universities run vacation
courses very suitable for single people. Write to
the university of your choice for information.

Two enterprising women run Travel
Companions* which aims to put single people
wanting to team up with others in the same

position in touch with each other. They'll send
you a form in return for a stamped addressed
envelope which you complete and return. The
form asks about your interests, where and
approximately when you'd like to go, your age and
other details. If there's someone else on their
books who's likely to be suitable, you meet before
making firm arrangements. This could be the
beginning of a lasting friendship, or a temporarily
convenient arrangement.

As you may have read on page 122, some
branches of the University of the Third Age*
arrange holidays for their members which is
another way of going on holiday with people you
know and like.

**Q** **Since I retired there are so many demands on
my time I just can't fit everything in. I want
to be useful, but I need some leisure time
too.**

**A** Almost all retired people meet this problem. They
probably expected to find plenty of time for
neglected interests and hobbies, but once the
local community knows they've retired, they find
their services in demand for all sorts of local
committees, running church bazaars, even baby-
sitting for grandchildren more often than they'd
actually bargained for.

You have to learn to say no. Perhaps you're not
as energetic as you used to be. So one reason for
not accepting everything you're offered would be
your need to take regular rests, whether an
afternoon snooze or a complete day off once or
twice a week. And you must actually plan to
spend a fixed, regular time on something you
enjoy – visiting art galleries, singing in a choir,
cinema-going or whatever. This will mean you
have begun to structure your time: you can
simply tell anyone who asks you to undertake
something that Tuesday afternoon or Friday

morning is your day for a certain activity, and
you're committed to it, and that except in
emergency, your arrangement gets priority. The
same applies to any voluntary work or other
commitment you have: you are available on that
day, and that day alone. As for baby-sitting, that
can be part of the pleasure of grandparenthood,
but it's only fair to yourself to have a basic and
limited commitment to that, too – say one
evening a week (not necessarily the same evening,
though this may be more convenient to both
parties) or one half-day to enable the children's
parents to do their shopping.

After a while you'll find your daily timetable
taking shape and you'll be only just as busy as
you want to be.

**Q** **I'm a middle-aged woman who feels she's just
drifting. I'm needed at home because I have
an elderly relative to care for as well as
teenage children. But I seem to fritter my
time away at coffee mornings, gossiping at
the shops, never really achieving anything.**

**A** Although your question is rather different from
any of the earlier ones in this chapter, you'll find
that in many of the answers there's something
that could apply to you. Despite your home ties
you could probably find time to undertake an
educational project, or join a voluntary
organization, or brush up old skills in preparation
for the time when you may be able to take a part-
or full-time job. Even though the demands upon
you may fluctuate, you, like the questioner
immediately above, can and should set aside
some fixed time when your priority is to go to a
class, attend the meeting of an organization, or
just read a book. Having a plan for the way you
spend your days can also help you to see that your
domestic responsibilities aren't getting on top of
you. You'll feel a lot better if you set aside certain

days or times for necessary housework and shopping and don't let them spill over into what should be leisure time. If you have something else planned, you won't be able to accept too many invitations for coffee or linger on too long when you do visit friends.

**Q** **I'm not looking forward to old age. How can I come to terms with the fact that I'm losing my looks, tiring more easily and getting so boring?**

**A** Some aspects of our older years just have to be accepted. Certainly if by 'losing your looks' you mean that you won't conform to the stereotype of the attractive or beautiful 20-year-old when you're 45, you're right. But if you eat and drink sensibly, don't smoke, take exercise and keep up your interests in people, work and leisure, you'll be an attractive person to know, whatever your years. You'll have a lot to contribute to the life around you, and in doing so, you'll forget to worry about the odd wrinkle or the rather thicker waistline. A lively interest in the world and keeping mentally alert will combat fatigue far more effectively than sitting around or popping pills.

It's usually bored people who are boring. If you never read anything absorbing, watch only undemanding TV, take no interest in what's going on in the world outside the home, accept other people's ideas without questioning the bases for their opinions, you'll probably be bored with life, and people will be bored with you.

Of course it isn't easy to change habits and behaviour, especially when the stereotype of older age is as all-pervading (and pernicious) as any other stereotype. But you can make an effort to get out and meet interesting people and undertake appealing activities. The local library could be your starting-point: ask to see their directory of associations and women's groups in the area, or consult *The Voluntary Agencies Directory* in the reference section for addresses of head offices of a huge variety of voluntary organizations that may have a branch near you. You may be interested in one of the traditional women's associations such as the Women's Institute* or the Townswomen's Guild,* but there are others, such as the National Women's Register,* or a local feminist or older women's group, or a conservation society, church organization or political party. There really is something for everyone, once you make up your mind to find it.

You have many years before you, and life can not only begin at 40, but at 45, 50 or beyond, if we choose to welcome all the opportunities on offer. A healthy, active, busy person doesn't feel her age and the time to prepare for a contented and productive future is *now*.

## Further reading

*Equal Opportunities: A Careers Guide* Anna Alston and Ruth Miller (Penguin)

*The Voluntary Agencies Directory* (Bedford Square Press)

*The Woman's Guide to Starting Your Own Business* Deborah Fowler (Grapevine/Thorsons)

*Women Can Return to Work* Maggie Steel and Zita Thornton (Grapevine/Thorsons)

# Useful addresses

## Britain

*Age Concern England* 60 Pitcairn Road, Mitcham, Surrey CR4 3LL (081-640 5431)

*Age Concern Scotland* 33 Carlisle Street, Edinburgh EH2 3DN

*Alzheimer's Disease Society* 158/160 Balham High Road, London SW12 9BN (081-675 6557/8/9)

*Amarant Trust* 14 Lord North Street, London SW1 (071-222 1220)

*Anorexic Aid* The Priory Centre, 11 Priory Road, High Wycombe, Bucks HP13 6SL

*Arthritis Care* 6 Grosvenor Crescent, London SW1X 7ER (071-235 0902)

*Arthritis and Rheumatism Council* 41 Eagle Street, London WC1R 4AR (071-405 8572)

*ASH Action on Smoking and Health* 5-11 Mortimer Street, London W1N 7RH (071-637 9843/6)

*Association of British Introduction Agencies* 29 Manchester Square, London W1 (071-938 1011)

*Association of Carers* 21-23 New Road, Chatham, Kent ME4 4JQ (0634 813981)

*Breast Care and Mastectomy Association* 26 Harrison Street, London WC1H 8JG (071-837 0908)

*Bristol Cancer Help Centre* Grove House, Cornwallis Grove, Clifton, Bristol BS8 4PG (0272 743216)

*British Acupuncture Association and Register* 34 Alderney Street, London SW1 4EU (071-834 1012)

*British Association of Cancer United Patients (BACUP)* 121/123 Charterhouse Street, London EC1M 6AA (071-608 1661)

*British Diabetic Association* 10 Queen Anne Street, London W1M 0BD (071-323 1531)

*British Red Cross Society* 9 Grosvenor Crescent, London SW1X 7EJ (071-235 5451)

*Centre for Policy on Ageing* 25-31 Ironmonger Row, London EC1V 3QP

*Chest, Heart and Stroke Association* Tavistock House N, Tavistock Square, London WC1H 9JE (071-387 3012)

*Co-operative Women's Guild* 342 Hoe Street, London E17 9PX (081-520 4902)

*Council for Voluntary Services — National Association* 26 Bedford Square, London WC1B 3HU (071-636 4066)

*Counsel and Care for the Elderly* Twyman House, 16 Barry Street, London NW1 9LR (071-485 1566)

*Cruse Bereavement Care* Cruse House, 126 Sheen Road, Richmond, Surrey TW9 1UR (081-940 4818)

*Elderly Accommodation Counsel (EAC)* 1 Durward House, 31 Kensington Court, London W8 5BH (071-937 8709)

*Fat Women's Support Group* c/o Beverly Duguid, 53 Sandbourne, Essex Gardens Centre, London W11 1DS (071-382 7513)

*Feminist Library and Information Centre* Hungerford House, Victoria Embankment, London WC2N 6PA (071-930 0715)

*Friends of the Earth* 26-28 Underwood Street, London N1 7JQ (071-490 1555)

*Help the Aged* 16-18 St James's Walk, London EC1R 0BE (071-253 0253)

*Institute for Complementary Medicine (ICM)* 21 Portland Place, London W1M 3AF (071-636 9534)

*Keep Fit Association,* 16 Upper Woburn Place, London WC1H 0QG (071-387 4349)

*Lesbian Line* BM Box 1514, London WC1 (071-251 6911)

*London Food Commission* 88 Old Street, London EC1V 9AR (071-253 9513)

*Marie Curie Memorial Foundation* 28 Belgrave Square, London SW1X 8QG (071-235 3325)

*Menopause Collective — see* Women's Health & Reproductive Rights Information Centre

*MIND (National Association for Mental Health)* 22 Harley Street, London W1N 2ED (071-637 0741)

*National Association of Grandparents* 8 Kirkley Drive, Ashington, Northumbria NE63 9RD

*National Association of Widows/Widows' Advisory Trust* 1st Floor, 14 Waterloo Street, Birmingham B2 5TX (021-643 8348)

*National Council for Voluntary Organizations* 26 Bedford Square, London WC1R 3HU (071-636 4066)

*National Institute of Adult Continuing Education* 19B de Montfort Street, Leicester LE1 7EG (0533 32472)

*National Osteoporosis Society (NOS)* P.O. Box 10, Barton Meade House, Radstock, Bath, Avon BA3 3YB (0761 551451)

*National Stepfamily Association* 162 Tenison Road, Cambridge CB1 2DP (0223 460312)

*National Women's Register* 245 Warwick Road, Solihull, West Midlands B92 7AH (021-706 1101)

*Older Feminist Network* c/o London Women's Centre, Wesley House, 4 Wild Court, London WC2B 5AU (071-831 7863)

*Older Lesbians' Network* Wesley House, Wild Court, London WC2

*Open University* Walton Hall, Milton Keynes MK7 6AA

*Patients' Association* Room 33, 18 Charing Cross Road, London WC2H 0HR (071-240 0671)

*Pre-Retirement Association* 19 Undine Street, London SW17 8PP (081-767 3225)

*Relate (National Marriage Guidance Council)* Herbert Gray College, Little Church Street, Rugby, Warwickshire CV12 3AP (0788 73241)

*Relaxation for Living* 29 Burwood Park Road, Walton-on-Thames, Surrey KT12 5LH

*Royal National Institute for the Blind (RNIB)* 224 Great Portland Street, London W1N 6AA (071-388 1266)

*Samaritans* 17 Uxbridge Road, Slough, Berks SL1 1SN (0753 32713/see telephone directory for local numbers)

*Shelter National Campaign for the Homeless* 88 Old Street, London EC1V 9HU (071-253 0202)

*Terence Higgins Trust* BM Aids, London WC1N 3XX (admin. 071-831 0330; helpline 071-242 1010)

*Townswomen's Guilds (National Union of)* Chamber of Commerce House, 75 Marbourne Road, Birmingham B15 3DA (021-456 3435)

*Travel Companions* 63 Mill Lane, London NW6 (071-431 1984)

*University of the Third Age (National Office)* 13 Stockwell Road, London SW9 9AU (071-737 2541)

*Volunteer Centre* 29 Lower King's Road, Berkhamsted, Herts HP4 2AB (04427 73311)

*Woman's Place* Hungerford House, Victoria Embankment, London WC2N 6PA (071-836 6081)

*Women's Aid Federation (England) Ltd* P.O. Box 391, Bristol BS99 7WS (0272 420611; helpline 0272 428368)

*Women's Health and Reproductive Rights Information Centre (WHRRIC)* 52-54 Featherstone Street, London EC1Y 8RT (071-251 6332/6580)

*Women's Institutes (National Federation of)* 39 Eccleston Street, London SW1 9NT (071-730 7212)

*Women's Therapy Centre (WTC)* 6 Manor Gardens, London N7 6LA (071-263 6200)

## United States

*AIDS Foundation Hotline* (415)863- AIDS or COYOTE) (415)552-1849

*Alzheimer's Disease and Related Disorders Association* 70 E. Lake St, Chicago, IL 60601 (800)621-0379

*American Foundation for the Blind* 15 W. 16th St, New York, NY 10011 (212)620-2172

*American Diabetes Association, National Service Center* 1660 Duke St, Alexandria, VA 22314 (800)232-3472

*The American Heart Association, National Center* 7320 Greenville Ave., Dallas, TX 75231 (214)373-6300

*The Arthritis Foundation* 1314 Spring St NW, Atlanta, GA 30309 (404)872-7100

*ASH (Action on Smoking and Health)* 2013 H. St NW, Washington, DC 20006 (202)659-4310

*The Cancer Information Service* (800)4-CANCER

*Children of Ageing Parents* 2761 Trenton Road, Levittown, PA 19056 (215)547-1070

*Federation of Parents and Friends of Lesbians and Gays Inc* P.O. Box 24565, Los Angeles, CA 90024

*Grandparents'-Children's Rights, Inc.* 5728 Bayonne Ave., Haslett, MI 48840 (517)339-8663

*National Cancer Survivors Network* P.O. Box 4543, Albuquerque, NM 87196 (505)268-7388

*National Council on the Ageing* 600 Maryland Avenue SW, West Wing 100, Washington, DC 20024 (202) 479-1200

*Older Women's League* 730 11th St NW, Suite 300, Washington, DC 20001 (202)783-6686

*Senior Action for a Gay Environment* P.O. Box 115, New York, NY 10023

*Stepfamily Association of America* 602 East Joppa Road, Baltimore, MD 21204 (301)823-7570

*Women's Association for Research in Menopause* 128 E. 56th St, New York, NY 10022

*Women's Health Information Center (US)* Boston Women's Health Book Collective, 47 Nichols Ave., Watertown, MA 02172

## Australia

*Australian Cancer Society Inc.* GPO Box 4708, Sydney, NSW 2001 (02) 211 2599

*Australian Council of Social Service* 8th Floor, 8-24 Kippax St, Surry Hills, NSW 2010 (02) 211 2599

*Australian Institute of Health* Bennett House, Hospital Point, Acton, ACT GPO Box 570, ACT 2601 (062) 43 5000

*Cardiac Society of Australia & New Zealand* 145 Macquarie St, Sydney, NSW 2000 (02) 27 4461

*Department of Community Services and Health* Suite 60 MG, Parliament House, Canberra, ACT 2600 (062) 77 7680

*Human Rights & Equal Opportunity Commission* Level 24, American Express Building, 388 George St, Sydney, NSW (02) 229 7600

*Ministry for Housing and Aged Care* Suite 48 M1, Parliament House, Canberra, ACT 2600 (062) 77 7220

*National Council of Women of Australia Inc.* PO Box 161, Stepney, SA 5069 (08) 271 0425

*National Heart Foundation of Australia* PO Box 2, Woden, ACT 2606 (062) 82 2144

*Voluntary Care Association of*
NSW & ACT Suite 1, Murray Arcade, 127-131 Burwood Rd, Burwood, NSW 2134 (02) 745 2999
Queensland PO Box 122, Boonah, Qld 4310 (075) 63 2607
S. Australia PO Box 327, Unley, SA 5061 (08) 373 0211
Tasmania (Inc.) 8 Blenheim St, Norwood, TAS 7250 (003) 44 8337

*Victoria* PO Box 47, Hawthorn, Vic 3122 (03) 819 3225
*W. Australia* PO Box 63, Cottesloe, WA 6011 (09) 383 1088
*Women's Health Care Association Inc.* 92 Thomas St, W.
 Perth, WA 6005 (09) 321 2833
*Women's Information Switchboard* 122 Kintore Ave.,
 Adelaide, SA 5000 (08) 223 2833

## Canada
*Alberta Women's Bureau* 1402 Centennial Building,
 10015-103 Ave., Edmonton, Alta T5J 0H1
*Canadian Advisory Council on the Status of Women* P.O.
 Box 1541, Station B., Ottawa, Ontario K1P 5R5
*Canadian Research Institute for the Advancement of
 Women* 151 Slater St, Suite 408, Ottawa, Ontario K1P
 5H3 (613) 563-0681/0682
*Health & Welfare Canada, National Day Care
 Information Centre,* Tunney's Pasture, Ottawa, Ontario
 K1A 1B5
*National Action Committee on the Status of Women* 40
 St. Clair Ave. E, Suite 306, Toronto, Ontario M4T 1M9
*National Council of Women of Canada* 270 MacLaren St,
 Room 20, Ottawa, Ontario K2P 0M3 (613) 233-4953
*New Brunswick Advisory Council on the Status of
 Women* 880 Main St, Moncton, New Brunswick E1C 1G4
*Ontario Status of Women Council* 700 Bay St, 3rd Floor,
 Toronto, Ontario M5G 1Z6
*Statistics Canada* Ottawa K1A 0T6 (613) 995-7808
*Women's Health Education Network* P.O. Box 1276, Truro,
 Nova Scotia B2N 5N2
*Women's Information & Referral Service* A Woman's
 Place, 1225 Barrington St, Halifax, Nova Scotia B3J 1YZ
*Women's Research Centre* 301-2515 Burrard St, Vancouver,
 British Columbia V6J 3T6
*Working Woman's Center* 1072A Bloor St W., Toronto,
 Ontario 1M6

## New Zealand
*Age Concern NZ Inc.* PO Box 1930, Wellington
*Department of Health* PO Box 5013, Wellington
*Mental Health Foundation of New Zealand Inc.* PO Box
 37438, Parnell, Auckland
*Ministry of Women's Affairs* 734-112 Box 10-049,
 Wellington

*National Council of Women of New Zealand (Inc)* PO Box 12117, Wellington North

*National Heart Foundation of New Zealand* PO Box 17160, Green Lane

*New Zealand Federation of Fitness Centres Inc.* PO Box 44029, Auckland

*Nutrition Society of New Zealand Inc.* Dept. of Food Technology, Massey University, Palmerston North

*Pacific Allied Women's Council* 63 Terry Street, Blockhouse Bay

*Society for Research on Women in New Zealand Ltd* PO Box 12270, Wellington North

*Women's Electoral Lobby (NZ Inc)* PO Box 24, Martinborough, Wairarapa

*Women's Studies Association (NZ)* PO Box 5067, Auckland

# General reading

*About Face: Towards a Positive Image of Housewives*
(Ontario Status of Women Council, Free)
*Canadian Women: Profile of Their Health* Louise Lapierre
(Statistics Canada, Health Division)
*The Complete Guide to Symptoms, Illness and Surgery*
Dr H. Winter Griffith (Thorsons)
*Equal Opportunities: A Careers Guide* Anna Alston and
Ruth Miller (Penguin)
*Family Doctor Home Adviser* Dr Tony Smith (Ed.) for the
British Medical Association (Dorling Kindersley)
*Growing Up Feminist* Joscelyne Scott (North Ryde, NSW:
Angus & Robertson)
*The Handbook of Complementary Medicine* Stephen
Fulder (Ed.) (Oxford)
*Having Families: Marriage, Parenthood and Social
Pressure in Australia* Lyn Richards (Ringwood, Victoria:
Penguin)
*The Health of Canadians* Report of the Canada Health
Survey, Catalogue 82-538 (Statistics Canada)
*Her Story: Australian Women in Print 1788-1975* Margaret
Bettison and Anne Summers (Sydney: Hale & Iremonger)
*In Her Prime: A New View of Middle-Aged Women* Judith
K. Browne (South Hadley, Massachusetts: Bergin &
Garvey)
*Listing of Women's Groups, Canada* Comprehensive
listing of names, addresses and telephone numbers of
women's groups across Canada (Secretary of State,
Women's Program, Free)
*Menopause: The Woman's View* Anne Dickson and Nikki
Henriques (Grapevine/Thorsons)

*The New Our Bodies, Ourselves* Boston Women's Health Book Collective (New York: Simon and Schuster/ London: Penguin)

*Older Women: Numerous and Needy* (New Brunswick Advisory Council on the Status of Women)

*Ourselves, Growing Older* Boston Women's Health Book Collective (Collins)

*Pink Pages: A Directory of Women's Rights in Australia* Barbara Bishop and Kerry Petersen (Melbourne: Penguin)

*The Seniors Boom* Leroy O. Stone and Susan Fletcher (Statistics Canada)

*Status of Day Care in Canada* National Day Care Information Centre (Health & Welfare Canada)

*The Voluntary Agencies Directory* (Bedford Square Press)

*A Wealth of Experience: The Lives of Older Women* Susan Hemmings (Ed.) (Pandora)

*When You're Alone: Helping You Cope in Widowhood* (Alberta Women's Bureau, Free)

*Women and Ageing* Louise Dulude (Canadian Advisory Council on the Status of Women)

*Women's Resource Catalogue* (Secretary of State, Women's Program USA)

# Index